EATING WITH
GOD'S FORK

EATING WITH
GOD'S FORK

How a Flawed Guy Backed Into
Starting Churches in South Sudan,
Sudan, and East Africa

MIKE CONGROVE

EATING WITH GOD'S FORK
How a Flawed Guy Backed Into Starting Churches in
South Sudan, Sudan, and East Africa

Cover Design by Jess LaGreca
Interior Layout and Design by Alice Briggs

ISBNs:
979-8-89165-222-4 *ebook*
979-8-89165-220-0 *Paperback*
979-8-89165-221-7 *Hardcover*

Published by:
Streamline Books
Kansas City, MO
streamlinebookspublishing.com

DEDICATION

For Ali, who's encouraged me to write this for years,
and who always says yes to adventure.

For Alexa, Weston, and Erin Kaya, here's most
of the story that's shaped your lives.

And for David Kaya, who's taught me everything I know about
Africa, and whom God used to give mission to my life.

CONTENTS

PART 1
MOSES

A Week at a Bible School in the World's Newest Country

A tukul, or traditional home, in South Sudan.

FROM ROOSTERS TO WORSHIP

THE CROWING DIDN'T awaken Moses. The clanging pots and pans did. And Mary Night's unmistakable laughter.

Roosters had been Moses's alarm clock since he was a little boy. He could tune them out, or he could use them to wake up when he needed to rise early. For those mornings, he'd tell himself to listen for the roosters just before falling to sleep. But on this particular Sunday, Moses relished an extra few moments in bed.

He'd only been at North East Africa Theological Seminary (NEATS) for a week, but he already knew the routine sounds of his new life. Mary Night was the head cook, and her boisterous laughter meant she was directing the younger women working in the kitchen, all of them carrying forty-plus-pound jerry cans of water on their heads. Jerry cans are what they called the plastic containers one might typically see strapped to a Land Cruiser, holding petrol or diesel fuel. Soon they'd be stirring *posha* over hot coals, preparing breakfast for the school. Posha was a staple at almost every meal. Sometimes made from maize, sometimes from sorghum or cassava, posha was boiled, its texture similar to grits but much firmer and with little to no flavor.

Still, Moses was grateful. At twenty-six years old, he was now sleeping in his first real bed. In fact, he spent an extra few seconds every morning in his dormitory bed thanking God for this opportunity, one he never wanted to take for granted. Moses oscillated from feeling overwhelmed to experiencing pure joy that his pastor had recommended he attend NEATS. He still couldn't believe that someone thought he'd be able to plant and lead a church someday.

The rooster crowed again. Moses smiled and got up. While NEATS was a seminary, no one had to worry about classes on Sundays.

But there was, of course, a worship service to get ready for.

Moses dressed himself, grabbed breakfast in the kitchen building, and walked a stone's throw length to the first flagship church in Kajo Keji, a church launched in 2002 with the help of a missionary from Kentucky.

Full-Circle Moments, David Discovers Moses

Moses loved Sundays, an inheritance from his mother, Beatrice. In a way, attending NEATS was a full-circle moment for him. Beatrice was the third of five wives to his father. All told, Moses was one of twenty-seven children (so far). But because his father couldn't support all his wives and children, only the first two wives still lived together with him. The other three wives left Moses's father's compound because they and their children were going hungry. Beatrice and Moses settled near her brother, who helped provide food. This also meant that Moses lived in a *tukul,* yet not the bigger tukul where his uncle slept. Moses's uncle told him one sign of manhood was the ability to build a tukul. In this part of South Sudan, they built their tukuls in a circular shape. They drove wooden poles into the ground and built a frame. Next, they formed the walls with mud mixed with straw, which hardened when it dried. Then, they would cover the cone-like roof structure with tall, dried grass. The thick mud walls and thatched roof kept the homes cool during the day. Moses's uncle had assigned the family to a smaller tukul built as a storage room for rice, maize, and potatoes. He slept on a plastic mat on a mud floor. He fought off bush rats who wanted their maize. He liked to hunt the bush rats out in the gardens and in the forest, but he resented their presence at night, disturbing his dreams. But at least the tukul was cool.

Moses's fortunes changed after Jesus changed his mother's life. In 2012, a schoolteacher named Jill from Plano, Texas, showed up at Beatrice's moonshine still. Jill shared Jesus's love with Beatrice, and she placed her faith in God. Beatrice began taking Moses to a church under a nearby mango tree that was about a fifteen-minute walk from their home. Soon, Moses placed his faith in Jesus and decided to follow him with all his heart. He loved Sunday worship, he loved hearing his mother sing—she had a beautiful voice—and he loved watching her dance. Eventually, the church asked Moses to lead songs and start a children's choir.

Then, one day, Pastor David Kaya showed up.

Moses knew Pastor David had sent Pastor Onesimus to start this church under a mango tree in Litoba years ago. Moses noted Pastor David observing him. David noticed how Moses made sure the pulpit was in place, how he shepherded the younger kids, and the zeal both Beatrice and he showed when they worshiped.

David asked Pastor Onesimus, "Tell me more about this young boy Moses. What is he like?"

Onesimus replied, "He is good, pastor. This one is very faithful even with no father around. He is sharp in his studies. He scored high on his last national exams. He wants to continue his schooling, but the family is struggling."

Pastor David paused, likely saying a quick prayer. "Pastor, you keep this quiet, but I will take care of Moses's school fees until he obtains his secondary school degree."

Onesimus smiled and slapped his hands together, then held out his right hand for David to shake. "Pastor, God is great all the time. Thank you, pastor." And he shook David's hand vigorously now with both hands wrapped around David's.

Onesimus reported Moses's progress to David, noting his continued zeal for the church and God as well as a natural ability to lead. Moses had begun gathering his peers every Saturday afternoon. He picked out five new tukuls each week for these small teams to visit and share the gospel. By the time Moses was twenty-five, he'd become the unofficial copastor of the church, a Timothy to Onesiumus's Paul (see Acts 16). That's when Onesimus brought Moses's name forward to the staff at NEATS for consideration as a student. Only a trusted, vetted pastor could refer a student to NEATS, which had been specifically created for leaders called to plant churches.

Based on David Kaya and Onesimus's high recommendations, Moses was accepted into NEATS.

When Moses heard the news, he was overjoyed. He couldn't believe how good God had been to him. He thanked God for his provision. Without his kindness, Moses knew he would have wound up as a subsistence farmer, a soldier, or a member of the rebel militia, which had actually heavily recruited him years ago.

And then he thought about the amazing ways God works across the globe. He knew that NEATS was started by a ministry called Empower One, and he knew that Jill's church donated to that ministry. The classroom he'd soon inhabit had been funded by the church that the woman who'd introduced his mother to Jesus attended.

Circle full.

Back at NEATS

Because of his singing and leadership abilities, the church worship leader quickly asked Moses to join Kajo Keji's adult choir. During this morning's worship service, he sang and danced for the Lord along with the choir. After wiping the sweat from his face, Moses took his seat in the flagship church. He was almost floating from the joy he derived from singing worship songs to God. A fellow student handed him his Bible. She'd been holding it for him because he didn't like to put his Bible on the floor. He wanted to keep it clean and free from scratches and abuse.

After a few announcements from Pastor Dima, Pastor David Kaya took the pulpit. Moses was excited to hear David preach. He revered David and thought of him as his spiritual father. After all, Pastor David had made it possible for Moses to finish secondary school. Moses listened to David preach from his favorite book, Revelation. And, just like each morning when he woke up in a real bed, Moses silently thanked God for where he sat today.

When church ended, Moses joined his fellow students in the kitchen. They lined up and washed their hands. One young lady poured water from a small plastic pitcher onto their hands, the water collecting in a large plastic basin.

"*Tinate*," Moses said, both thanking the young lady and indicating for her to stop pouring.

After washing, each student took a plastic bowl. Moses grabbed a blue one, about seven inches in diameter, with a small lip for a rim. The young ladies, under Mary Night's supervision, ladled posha, rice, and then beans into Moses's bowl. Posha filled the belly, and Moses used it to soak up the moisture from the beans. If they were fortunate enough to have a protein, mostly fish or chicken, the ladies would always cook those in a stew, which Moses would also let soak into his posha.

He walked to a nearby tree where the compound's caretaker had installed benches exactly like the pews at Moses's home church. A few chickens pecked at the ground nearby. Two goats scratched their sides on the kitchen wall. Other students squeezed in. They each ate with their right hands. As Pastor David Kaya approached, he laughed and bellowed, "You are eating with God's fork today!"

After eating, Moses took his full belly back to the dorm. He loved that NEATS provided meals. He carried in his shoes. Everyone was required to remove their shoes when entering the dorm. With over forty guys in the dorm—a large open room with bunk beds—everyone had to cooperate to keep things as clean as possible. Back by his bed, he changed out of his church clothes, hanging and folding every item carefully, and put on an old T-shirt and shorts. He walked to the dorm entrance and slid his feet into his slides. From there, it was a short walk to the football pitch.

Moses couldn't afford a pair of football boots, or shoes, yet, but he'd walked barefoot his entire life. His feet were plenty tough. Young guys had arrived from three nearby *payams* for the weekly Sunday football games. Payams were sections of the county, and within each payam were *bomas*, another name for villages. Some teams had already formed and always played together. Moses, new to the church and NEATS compound, had to find a team. They had two balls. One was in pretty good shape. They saved that one for more important, or official, matches. The one Moses played with today was held together with tape and string. The matches ran from about 2 p.m. until 6 p.m. because at 6, David and Edward wanted everyone back in the church for evening Bible study.

After the evening Bible study, Moses picked up a five-gallon bucket and walked over to a water spigot.

"Thank you, Lord, for easy water. This is a blessing." Moses prayed a prayer of thanks every time he used the spigot.

Instead of the large metal India Mark II hand pumps Moses had used in his home village, which were a full kilometer's walk from his tukul, all Moses had to do here was turn a valve. David Kaya had drilled a water well for the compound. He'd also installed a solar-powered pump that pumped water to a thirty-foot high, twenty-thousand-liter water tank. From this tank, five water distribution points were spread throughout the compound.

Moses lugged his full bucket to the small outdoor shower reserved for male students. He opened the corrugated metal door framed with wood. He placed his flashlight on one of the wooden support beams and his bucket on the concrete floor. It was sloped a bit so the water would flow into a drain at the back of the shower. At home, his shower had been floored with rocks. They'd hung a plastic tarp stamped with the United Nations name and logo around the rocks for privacy. His uncle had picked up a few tarps from a refugee camp in Uganda.

After his bucket shower, Moses joined Sunday—he was from the Murle tribe—near a lantern. Moses opened his Bible to 1 Corinthians 5 and started to write his outline and observations for class tomorrow. Sunday turned the lantern off, and they sat and talked. Their eyes adjusted to the darkness. Moses looked up and took in a half-moon and stars that filled the sky and listened to the chirping of crickets. He felt so good.

The day had started with worship and Pastor David's preaching, then a good meal, exercise, and competition with new friends, and had ended with that clean feeling after a shower when the breeze blows over your skin. God and life were good. After praying with Sunday, Moses crawled into his real bed with a real mattress and a real pillow and slipped off to sleep.

He told himself, *Listen for the roosters tomorrow, Moses. You don't want to be late for class.*

WHAT IS DISCIPLESHIP, REALLY?

THE ROOSTERS SCREECHED their morning worship song around 4:30 a.m., but Moses told himself to wait to rise until 6. However, Abraham, his bunkmate from the Dinka tribe, woke him by talking to him as if he were awake. "Why are you not awake, my Kuku friend? We Dinka rise early to care for our cows. I will train you to become a Dinka," Abraham said with a big smile.

Even as Moses lay in the top bunk, the six-foot-ten-inch Abraham towered over him.

"Thank you, Lord, for my real bed and for this opportunity." Moses prayed, then jumped out of bed.

Chapel started at 7, and class days were always packed and rigorous. Even though Moses had just begun attending NEATS, he'd memorized the schedule:

Chapel at 7 a.m., then straight to class at 8 a.m. Only after class did they eat breakfast: almost always two pieces of cassava and a cup of tea. That was at 10 a.m., then they went back to class at 11 a.m. A lunch break was at 1 p.m., where every day Abraham would ask Moses, "Is today rice and beans or beans and rice?" They were back in class at 3 p.m. for their afternoon session, then had a break at 5 p.m. until dinner at 7 p.m. (Typically rice and beans. Sometimes beans and rice.) At 8 p.m. was evening chapel, then free time or study time at 9 p.m. and lights out at 10 p.m.

Moses loved the structure of it, something he hadn't experienced before attending NEATS.

After dressing, Moses grabbed a short stick. He walked outside and used the stick's flayed end to brush his teeth. After splashing water on his face, he swung by the kitchen, hoping there were leftovers from the previous night. Victory! The ladies had sat out a large metal pot with rice the children didn't finish, which was rare. Moses only took a small scoop with his hand so there'd be enough for the other students and the kids who roamed the school's grounds. Real breakfast was at 10, so this was a treat.

He walked into the church where they held chapel each morning and grabbed a seat. Professor Dominic Eruaga, who taught theology and oversaw the school's sixteen extension centers, stood at the front. When he saw Moses, he waved him up and told him, "Please lead *precisely* three songs." Dominic was warm, fun, and a great teacher, but he was also tough and could be directive. He limited Moses to three songs, knowing Moses could easily sing six or seven songs in a row. Unlike Sunday mornings, these chapel worship sessions were a cappella and unplanned.

Moses asked, "Does anyone have any song requests?" Abraham's long arm shot up. With a huge smile, he asked to sing "My Hope Is Built on Nothing Less," in Arabic. Moses complied, leading the first song in Arabic, the second in English, and the third in his language of Kuku. Fortunately, the church had Kuku hymn books so that everyone could sing along. The school taught and operated in English, but with sixty-four tribes in South Sudan alone, plus students from Sudan, the Democratic Republic of Congo (DR Congo), and Uganda, they had to stick to only a few languages for singing.

Students took turns leading the devotional time, and the professors would debrief with those students after they led. They'd coach them on what they did well and where they could improve. The faculty took seriously that they were not only teaching the Bible and theology but also shaping future church leaders. Everything the students did mattered. In these debriefs, the faculty were modeling for the students how to disciple.

Ding, from the Nuer tribe, rose to lead the devotional. "Please, everyone, open your Bibles to Proverbs chapter nineteen verse eleven." He paused, giving everyone time to find the verse. Then he read, "Good sense makes one slow to anger, and it is his glory to overlook an offense."

Ding was tall like Abraham. They represented the two dominant tribes in South Sudan: Dinka for Abraham, Nuer for Ding. In fact, their tribes were the primary antagonists in the most recent civil war.

Ding continued, "Brothers and sisters, this is my second year at NEATS. We are beginning our second week of these good teachings by our most excellent faculty. Let this verse sink into your heart. Let us receive this glory by overlooking offenses. We are bunking together, eating together, studying together, and even playing games together. Remember to be slow to anger with one another. Even my brother here, Abraham. Even us. We reject this war between our tribes. Because of what Christ has done in our hearts, we are brothers and are one in Christ."

Moses drew out the pencil he had tucked in his shirt's front pocket and carefully underlined the verse in his Bible. Ding took the students from Proverbs to John 15, imploring them to be like Jesus and to love one another like Jesus loved them.

By 8 a.m., Moses needed to be in his classroom, seated, and ready to learn. The school provided him with a notebook and a pencil. He had a Bible that an American short-term missionary had given his mother. He couldn't wait to get one of the larger study Bibles that every NEATS graduate received on graduation day. He also knew exactly where his certificate would hang: in his mother's tukul. And he couldn't wait to wear those graduation robes with necklaces of flowers. But that was a year or two away.

Today, he hustled to his classroom, barely making it before the class opened with singing and prayer, the way every class began. Then Professor Idrifua Patrick stood up at the front of the room and continued his survey of 1 Corinthians. Moses leaned in, not wanting to miss a second of insight.

Moses lingered after class. "Professor Patrick, I am struggling with how to organize my notes. What is the best way to follow your teaching and record them in my notes?"

Professor Patrick showed him how to create sections on each page to more quickly organize and access key information. This caused Moses to be late to lunch. He had to stand and wait for the first batch of students to finish eating so the ladies could rinse those plates for Moses's turn to load up on rice and beans.

Moses loved the new friends he was making at NEATS. He listened when Mawa John Liki, the school's president, encouraged the students to make friends outside of their tribe during his orientation. While Moses felt closest to other Kukus, he made a point to eat and spend time with Abraham, the Dinka, and Sunday, the Murle. And everyone loved Isaac from Yambio, a Zande. He, along with the other Southerners, were glad the six Darfurians were in his class as well. Everyone loved that the former Muslims had found Jesus and were learning with them.

But Moses's classical Arabic was rudimentary. He only knew Juba Arabic, which didn't fully translate, and the Darfurians' English wasn't great either. He admired them for how they'd spend hours with their English tutor after a grueling full day of classes. Five of them had attended *madrassas*, Muslim religious schools, when they were young. In addition to English, they were having to learn how to think about what they were learning and not focus on only memorizing their lessons. Moses was impressed that four of the five had memorized the entire Koran by the time they were fourteen. Adam, the fifth one, took until he was sixteen. He recounted the daily beatings he would endure until he could recite the entire book.

I Can Do That

At 5 p.m., Moses walked to a specific *lulu*, or shea nut, tree. Visiting professor Emmanuel Lomo, whom everyone called Emma, sat under that tree, along with Moses's friends Abraham, Sunday, Isaac, and Martha, one of the women students and another member of the Nuer tribe.

Once the students were settled, Professor Emma said, "I'm going to disciple you this entire year."

Moses thought, *I've read about the disciples who followed Jesus, but I don't know what Professor Emma means.*

The professor saw Moses's look of concern, and his wasn't the only one. Before anyone replied, Professor Emma said, "Here's what I mean. It's very simple. We'll meet under this lulu tree every Monday at this time. We'll discuss a short passage from the Bible. Then I'm going to ask you questions about your life. Then you can ask me questions about anything. You see? This is simple."

The students nodded their heads.

Moses thought, *That's discipleship? That's it? I can do that.*

But then Professor Emma went deeper. He said, "On one of your off days, I want each of you to spend time with me at my home to see how I treat my wife and family. And you'll come with me to visit widows in the community and share the gospel with others there too."

The students looked excited at the prospect of visiting Professor Emma's home, but some seemed concerned about sharing the gospel with strangers. Moses felt the opposite. His Saturday outreaches at home had him confident with the practice, but watching a husband and wife interact in their home as Christians made him, surprisingly, a little nervous.

The professor continued, "Also, when you lead chapel, I'll be the one who gives you feedback. I can help you prepare to give the devotional as well."

Every student smiled at that.

"Lastly, and this is important: Don't just listen to me. Watch me. Copy my behavior. It's just like the apostle Paul wrote in 1 Corinthians 11:1: 'Be imitators of me, as I am of Christ.'"

Moses knew he could do that.

The professor wrapped up his lesson for the day, then the dinner bell rang. He grabbed Moses by his shoulder and held him back for a second. Professor Emma said, "Meet me at the radio station tomorrow night for your 5 p.m. break. Bring your class notebook. I hope you've taken good notes on what you've learned about 1 Corinthians so far, enough to talk about it for twenty minutes at least. You're going live on air."

MOONSHINE TO RADIO MINISTRY

CHAPEL LET OUT a bit early that morning. Moses was grateful he didn't have to rush. When he stepped out of the church, he looked across the grounds beyond the kitchen. A woman caught his eye. She was sitting under a tree, in the shade, with David Kaya, Edward Dima, and a third man he didn't know standing over her. Her dress was filthy. Even from this distance, he could see how ratty and dirty it had become. Who knows what color it was originally? Now it was various shades of brown. He saw her unkempt hair. He knew something was wrong with her. Here, unless a woman's hair was properly fixed, braided, or straightened nicely, they always covered their heads. The only exception was if they were working in the garden. Even then it was rare.

Pastor David and the other men had their hands on her shoulders and head and were praying for her. Just then, Professor Dominic walked by. Moses touched his arm and asked, "Professor, what is happening with that lady?"

He pointed in her direction. "That woman arrived here last night. Her husband and his brother carried her here for prayer. She has a demon and is terrorizing her home and community. If the pastors cannot cast out the demon, you students will all take turns praying for her twenty-four hours a day until God delivers her."

Moses was filled with compassion. He hoped the pastors' prayers would relieve her, but he also hoped God would use him to pray for her freedom.

Moses would be stunned after seeing that it took five days of nonstop prayer for the demons to submit to God and leave this woman. Pastor Kaya called the students together and explained how rare it was for it to take so many days of prayer. He expressed his gratitude at everyone's perseverance. If Moses knew then that one of the professors at NEATS would marry this woman a few years later, he might have fainted.

Something about how this woman looked reminded Moses of his mother Beatrice before she'd met Jesus.

Beatrice's Story

Moses remembered his mother telling him how she hated brewing alcohol. She hated how it smelled and hated that his father's desertion had put her in this position. She hated it most for what it did to the men in her village, and plenty of the women as well.

In the refugee camp in the previous war, she recalled to Moses how she observed some nongovernmental organization (NGO) workers drinking a few beers on Friday nights. What she observed in her village with her sorghum wine looked nothing like that. For the equivalent of about a US dollar, she'd pour two pints of the moonshine in whatever container a buyer could scrounge up. She never observed any of her customers only taking a few sips or having the pints only on a week-end night. She watched them consume the high-percentage alcohol almost immediately until they stumbled to a ditch or an empty field to pass out. After coming to faith, Moses remembered an American Christian named Diana inviting his mother to a workshop on trauma. That's where she learned why her former customers drank: to silence the effects of their trauma from wars, sexual violence, and living just to survive.

Beatrice was so grateful that God had brought that first American lady to her tukul. Moses was too. He hoped he could meet her and thank her someday. Immediately after learning about Jesus, all Beatrice wanted was to learn as much as she could about God. Every week, she was excited to go to the church and worship and learn. Moses would watch her wash her one good dress on Fridays, along with a collared shirt she'd found for him. She always washed these on Friday mornings so they would have both Friday and Saturday to dry on the line. On Saturday evenings, she took red-hot coals from the cooking fire and placed three or four into a small compartment in her iron. Fully heated, she'd make sure Moses's shirt was nicely pressed for Sunday.

On Sunday mornings, Beatrice and Moses would walk on the footpaths through the gardens of cassava, maize, sweet potatoes, and onions to the small church under a large mango tree. Pastor Onesimus had driven Y-shaped wooden stakes into the ground and then laid logs inside the Y shape to make two sets of pews. He used a hammer and nails to put together a thin pulpit from scrap boards. It was too tall and covered his face when he stood behind it to preach. Beatrice leaped at the chance to volunteer to care for the cloth covering for the pulpit. She'd always make sure it was clean, keeping it bright white. She sewed a red cross on its bottom third. She made sure Moses brought it to church. She gave him the job of laying it over the top of the pulpit. She knew that big responsibility made him feel special.

At church, the oldest boys took charge of the drum. A crafts-man had covered it with smooth goatskin on both ends and kept it tight with thin leather bands strung around the side. A skinny seventeen-year-old was the number one drummer at the church. He always had slides for his feet. (A lot of kids lacked shoes. Beatrice worked hard to keep at least a pair of slides on Moses's feet.) The drummer kept a stick in one hand and a piece of thick rubber in the other. The rubber piece was about the thickness of a car tire, and it was only about an inch and a half wide by about nine inches long. Depending on the song, he'd switch, use both, or only use his hands. Sometimes, they'd get so caught up in worship that he would look to another teenager to come and take a turn on the drum because he'd need to rest for a song.

One of the deaconesses would start the worship, calling out a line, and the congregation would respond in song. With no hymnals and low literacy, it helped the congregation learn the songs. Moses knew Beatrice was so excited to sing and worship, she could rarely make it past the first song without jumping to the front of the church. She felt so alive worshiping and singing that she would move out from the pew, dance to the front, and sing with the other ladies doing the same. As she grew in her faith and gained more confidence, she, along with about a dozen other women, would come to church dressed the same: blue headwrap, white robe with a blue cross sewn on the chest, and a thin blue cord around their waists. Some members called them deaconesses, but most just referred to them as the ladies of the church.

Moses watched Beatrice wave a wooden cross as she danced and sang. On many mornings, using her other hand, she'd wave a hand-kerchief blazing with colors over the women or young people as they sang, danced, and worshiped. Moses knew she felt him watching. She was so proud when the pastor asked him to lead songs and, eventually, to train all the children to become a children's choir. She loved seeing him use his gifts to serve the church.

Talk Radio, NEATS Style

As soon as his Tuesday class let out at 4:55 p.m., Moses made a beeline for the radio station. Even though the knot in his stomach hadn't lessened since Professor Emma had told him he'd be radio preaching that night, Moses was still excited for the experience. He didn't want to be late, and the radio tower was about five football fields away from his classroom. Sweating inside and out, Moses ran.

Pastor David had converted the radio station from a room that had previously been a sewing center, an internet cafe, and the head-quarters of a British aid NGO. In an age of podcasts, some American short-term missionaries thought it odd to have a radio station. But in South Sudan, terrestrial radio was still effective. Almost every home in the county had radios, and Pastor David had seen many people show up to church because they'd heard about Jesus on his local station. They broadcast every day from 6 a.m. until 9 p.m. Tonight, Moses and Professor Emma would take 5:30 p.m. to 6:30 p.m.

Moses had never worn headphones like these before. They were large and covered his ears completely. The radio station manager had to keep encouraging him to put his mouth closer to the microphone. Emma seemed natural and comfortable. He'd clearly done this many times before.

Emma got the show rolling. "Ladies and gentlemen of Kajo Keji county, we are so happy to present our Bible teaching to you this evening. If you have a Bible, we will be in first Corinthians chapter five. If you do not have a Bible, no problem. You just listen. We will read everything you need to hear to you for your utmost convenience. This evening, I have a special guest. His name is Moses Mansom Lubang. I will begin by reminding everyone about who these people called Corinthians are, and who this man Paul is in the Bible. After some time, our young NEATS student, Moses, will really give you a good teaching."

The knot in Moses's stomach tightened even more. He spread his notes on the table under his microphone. Then he heard Emma say, "Now please pay close attention to my new disciple, Moses, and let us all hear him teach the word of God to us. Thank you, Moses, you go ahead."

As Moses went through his notes, he hoped his mother had her radio on at her tukul, hearing her son's voice broadcast across their entire county.

WEDNESDAY

JESUS VS. WITCH DOCTORS

ON WEDNESDAY, THE NEATS faculty changed the day's schedule and ended the afternoon class at 4 p.m. While Moses liked the structure, he was still adjusting to keeping precise time. At home, no one worried about keeping time. If Moses needed to be in the garden or even at church, it was no issue if he delayed because he was caught up in conversation with his brother or a neighbor. At NEATS, the faculty ran the schedule with precision. Everything started at a specific time, and you were expected not only to be on time but to show up a little early. This was the culture and legacy NEATS's first president, Edward Dima, instilled. Edward was insistent that at NEATS, everyone kept time. He was teaching them how to organize themselves, skills they would need when leading multiple churches in their futures.

Pastor Onesimus had told Moses one thing he loved about NEATS was that it involved a lot of practicums. While Moses enjoyed the lectures and reading, he'd been looking forward to his first practicum in the field. He appreciated that he would get to *do* ministry as much as learn about it. At 4:30, they gathered in front of their dorm. Andrew Yunda, a pastor from the area and now a NEATS adjunct professor of the New Testament, walked in front of the gathered students. He had a small backpack slung around his right shoulder.

Andrew talked with a lisp and had a good-natured attitude about his nickname: the Rat Eater. Rather than feel insecure about it, he'd leaned into it and embraced it. He'd ask anyone brave enough to use it around him if they wanted to join him for a bush rat feast. He seemed to genuinely enjoy a roasted bush rat served on a wooden skewer. He said he preferred bush meat to pork or beef. No one knew if he was serious or not.

"Attention, students!" Andrew barked. He clapped his hand three times. Once everyone quieted, he continued in a softer tone. "Today, we are heading to Lira. Pastor Alex was a student like you two years ago. He planted a very nice church, but he is requesting our help to encourage his church. You, my tall friend." He pointed to Abraham. "You pray for us, then let us all load into the truck."

Abraham said, "Let us pray," and led the students in prayer for the mission.

Lagu, the chief driver and the best mechanic perhaps in the entire country, saw his queue and positioned the flatbed lorry in front of the students. In South Sudan, they followed British English and called the big trucks lorries. Lagu sat in the driver's seat with sunglasses on, listening to the diesel engine idle. The large bed of the big truck had been outfitted with walls and metal arches. Moses learned that at other times, they'd cover the bed with canvas and fill it with supplies and Jesus Film equipment, which included a projector, amplifier, poles and a screen, speakers, and a generator. The organization that supplied the equipment, the Jesus Film Project, originally made the film (*JESUS*) in 1979. Since then, billions of people had watched this word-for-word account of the book of Luke in over two thousand languages. But the teams setting up the film viewings didn't give that much thought. They just loved that it honored Scripture, and they saw that a live movie was always a powerful draw. And most of them just referred to it as "the Jesus Film." A team would live out of that truck for weeks in an area, sharing the gospel. Moses had heard how many people had put their faith in Christ from these outreaches, particularly in the refugee camps in northern Uganda. Moses hoped he'd get invited to one of those missions. Living with your brothers and sisters on mission out of that big truck sounded like a great adventure.

The big truck loaded, Lagu released the air brakes, put the truck in gear, and slowly maneuvered it down roads that resembled dry creek beds more than actual roads. Lira wasn't a far drive: about thirty minutes from the dorm. As soon as the ladies from the church saw the truck, they began dancing toward it, waving handkerchiefs and trilling—a distinctive sound Moses had heard all his life. The women would vibrate their tongues while letting out a high-pitched musical sound, a signal of pure joy and excitement.

Once Lagu came to a full stop, the students jumped down over the back gate or climbed out of the sides, using the tires as ladders. This afternoon, a teenager was beating a drum under a large mango tree with surrounding logs for pews, signaling it was the church site.

Everyone began clapping with the drum, swinging their arms and dancing. Moses called out a line to a song and everyone responded. Worship began. A few curious neighbors appeared, smiling. With the pounding of the drum, the singing, and the worship, a joy and energy began to radiate from this church under a mango tree.

Pastor Andrew quieted the group. "Dear most gracious King of glory, we magnify your name, oh Lord. We know every good thing comes from your hand, gracious Father." Andrew continued, thanking God, acknowledging God's greatness, and praying for these students and the community.

When he opened his eyes, he paused before speaking, "Students of NEATS, this is my good friend and an alumnus of your same school, Keji Alex. Pastor Alex finished his studies two years ago and a committee of church leaders sent him here, to Lira, to start this church."

Off to the side, one of the students translated from English into Kuku for the church members.

Before Andrew could continue, the students broke out in applause.

"Students, today is a good lesson for you. We keep our churches strong. We all work together. This pastor came for meetings last month. He and his deacons shared with us that they were feeling a little bit down. Today, you are here to give them a push. God has sent you to be like Barnabas to Lira. Today, you are all encouragers!"

Pastor Alex smiled. His deacons clapped and shook one another's hands.

Andrew quickly organized the students into teams of three. "Each team, choose now a team leader. You need a team leader." After seeing team leaders emerge, he said, "Now choose one member to record a report for your team. Team leaders, pray for your team and for your time of outreach." Then Andrew asked Alex to send them in different directions to visit homes in that community.

Respect the Chief

South Sudanese love having people visit their homes. In their culture, it is an honor to host a visitor.

Moses's team was led by James, another Dinka but not nearly as tall as Abraham. Martha, the scribe, accompanied them. They approached their first home, which consisted of four tukuls surrounded by a fence with flowering shrubs. Plastic and handmade wooden chairs appeared from nowhere.

Without daring to make eye contact, a teenage girl told Moses, "You sit."

The women laid a tarp on the ground, took their shoes off, and sat on the ground. James broke the ice. "Did you get your potatoes started?"

A woman in her mid-twenties responded. "Yes, pastor. It is good you came now. We are resting while it is quite hot. When the sun goes down a bit, we will return to our garden to keep cultivating when it is cooler."

After the initial get-to-know-you discussion, James asked, "Would you like to know why we are here visiting your home?"

James saw the group, which now included several men and teenage boys, nod their heads yes. James began with the creation of the world and Adam and Eve, and how after they ate the forbidden fruit, sin, pain, disease, and violence entered the world. James understood on an intrinsic level that he operated in a power culture. When he translated for short-term American missionaries, he would watch their eyes go wide when he discussed witch doctors, ancestral spirits, and the animistic practices he grew up with that were still prominent throughout South Sudan. Because of these practices, he liked to start by telling the story of creation. He wanted to establish that God created everything and holds ultimate power over everything.

James explained God establishing the need for a blood sacrifice for the bad things people did. But ultimately, what God really cared about, even in the time of animal sacrifices, was people's hearts. Then, he bridged to the story of Jesus, making sure to start at Jesus's miraculous virgin birth and how amazing it was that he would leave heaven to be born among animals.

He was careful to explain that Jesus never did anything wrong and how he became the one ultimate sacrifice for everything bad ever done from creation to the future. He described Jesus's death on the cross and his burial, and then he became animated when describing Jesus's resurrection from the dead.

He paused there and asked the group, which had grown by five more neighbors since he'd begun talking, "Has a witch doctor ever brought someone back to life?"

There were a few quiet noes and shaking of heads.

James said, "That's right—only God has the power of life and death."

After describing Jesus more, James paused again. He asked, "Would any of you like to follow Jesus completely with everything in you? Allow him to take away all the bad things you've ever done and ever will do? And to come into his heavenly kingdom here on earth? Would you stop with the visits to the witch doctors and the sacrifices to family and area spirits?" James didn't use the word *sin* because, for many in the villages, it had no meaning. He stuck with "bad things" instead.

There was a long pause.

James, Moses, and Martha knew exactly why everyone was quiet: An elderly man had joined the group. He was thin, with gray stubble on his face, wearing a worn *kanzu*, which had long pants and a shirt that hung below his knees when he stood. The kanzu flowed and was nice when the weather was hot. He carried a finely carved staff about fourteen inches long. That was the team's tell. The staff indicated he was a chief. It was unlikely he was the paramount chief, but he was a chief in this area and he commanded respect.

His stature also meant no one would answer James until the chief spoke first.

After a long silence, the elderly chief spoke, with long pauses separating his every sentence. "Thank you, young man of God, for coming to this home and to my people. I am appreciating you for telling us the story from this Bible. When I was young during the last war, I prayed in a church in Rhino camp. Even though I prayed in that church, I did not understand the teachings. I did not know about this Jesus. He is very powerful and wonderful. Young man of God, you are very good. I will consider this story you have spoken of Jesus.

"It is a big thing for God to die for me and for us. And, you are right, young man of God. Even me, I used to be a witch doctor. No one has brought someone back from the dead. This is big power. You three come back to my home next week. We will take tea and talk more at that time."

Then he waved his hand across the group and said, "Be free to make your own decisions."

Rebecca, one of the women on the mat, spoke up. She spoke so quietly that it was hard to make out her words. As she spoke, she moved one hand through the pile of drying okra on the mat, flipping the cut pieces and moving them around. With the other, she balanced her baby while he nursed. "I am a Christian. I prayed in church when I was young."

Martha took the lead with the young lady. "Yes, momma, I hear you are a Christian, but are you born again?" It was a funny question, and when Americans were with the teams it always surprised the Americans when someone would ask that question.

Rebecca replied, "No, I am not born again."

This is common. Many South Sudanese took Christian names and completed a training around the age of thirteen in a church. The leaders of those churches told them they were Christians. Rarely had they learned anything about Jesus or the gospel.

Martha asked her, "Sister, what do you think of what my brother James has shared about Jesus with you?"

Rebecca replied, "Yes, I want to know this Jesus."

Martha looked around and asked, "Would any of you like to follow Jesus like this lady here?"

Three hands went up. Martha looked at Moses. She asked him to lead them to pray in their mother tongue, the Kuku language. They prayed and Martha hugged all the ladies. The men who prayed broke out in big smiles. Martha wrote each person's name down. She took the phone numbers of the two who had phones. She told them, "Someone from the church will come here tomorrow at the same time to begin teaching the Bible. Everyone is welcome to hear the teaching."

Moses asked the group, "Would anyone like prayer for anything in your life?"

After a pause, a middle-aged man wearing a worn, white tank top spoke up. "We need peace in our country. Please pray for peace."

Then one of the ladies, leaning back on the mat on the ground, pointed to a teenage boy lying beside her. "This one has malaria. He is very weak, and he has a fever. Please, pastor, pray for him."

Moses got up from his chair and walked over to the boy. He laid his hands on him and prayed. When he finished, Martha was right by him, holding the boy's arm, and she prayed as well.

Moses addressed the group. "God heals in his own timing. In my village when we pray for this, sometimes God heals that same day. Other times after a few days. And there are times God allows suffering for a bigger purpose."

The lady on the mat by the sick boy seemed to agree, "Mmm, yes, pastor, that is true."

In a power culture, witnessing God's power often drew skeptical people to follow Jesus.

The ladies poured water from a five-gallon yellow jerry can into a glass. Moses drank the entire glass quickly, then handed it back. They refilled the glass, then James and then Martha each drank water from the same glass. They returned to discussing cultivating, and the group indicated it was time to return to their gardens. Martha spoke up. "Tomorrow, someone from Pastor Alex's church will come to this home to continue teaching you all the Bible."

They said their goodbyes.

When they returned to the mango tree church, Martha gave the pastor a piece of lined notebook paper with each person's name and the two phone numbers.

The pastor replied, "Thank you, sister. We will send a deacon team to this home."

The remaining teams arrived. Andrew signaled to Alex, and he began to sing. Everyone joined. They only sang one song, this one a slower hymn: "Blessed Assurance."

Andrew looked the students over and said, "Team leaders, quickly give a report."

Seventeen people had made a profession of faith in Jesus. Pastor Alex and his deacons were on fire tonight and couldn't wait to follow up the next day. Before their visit, he was depressed, lonely, and discouraged. Now, Alex expected he would barely sleep that night because of how excited he felt.

It was getting dark, so after closing in prayer, the students all shook Alex's and each deacon's hand. Then they climbed aboard the lorry for the ride back to the dorm.

Moses stood overlooking the cab of the truck at the front of the bed. The breeze felt good on his face, and he could hear the cicadas and crickets buzzing in the forest. He realized that he loved introducing people to Jesus. He still felt a few butterflies at the thought of going out again, but he also felt excited and full of joy. He told God again, "Thank you, Lord. I am so thankful to be at NEATS."

THURSDAY

MALARIA AND THE AMERICANS

WITH ROOSTERS CROWING and pots and pans clanging, students slid out of their beds to make 7 a.m. chapel. Moses thanked God for his bed yet again, then swung his legs over the side and dropped to the floor. Now he stood over Abraham's bottom bunk.

Abraham not only had his sheet over him, but he'd found a gray, wool blanket and had it wrapped tightly around him. This concerned Moses because he never woke before Abraham, and it was plenty warm in the dorm. The construction team had done a nice job creating vents at the top for airflow, but it was still built from concrete blocks that would warm during the day and keep that heat throughout the night. It was as cool as it would get in the morning, but rarely did one need a wool blanket.

Moses nudged Abraham. He woke and looked at Moses. His eyes were red, and he started to shiver.

Moses said, "You have malaria."

Abraham nodded.

"Okay, my tall friend. I will help you today. You lay here. I will get you water to drink. On my first break, I will go to the pharmacy for medicine for you."

Abraham mumbled back, "No, I want injection."

In Abraham's home village, the people only trusted injections. His mother had told him to avoid pills and always ask for an injection. It went back to when the first vaccinations arrived in their village. It formed this conviction.

"No, my friend." Moses replied. "I know your people only accept injections, but these pills work the same. You must trust me on this. I will get you the right pills and they will work just like an injection."

"*Shukran*, my brother." Abraham thanked him in Arabic, closed his eyes, and rolled over.

Moses ate his breakfast quickly and used the remainder of that break time to walk to the pharmacy. The entire compound was about forty acres in the form of a rectangle. The dorm and kitchen were on one end and the pharmacy on the other. David Kaya had put the pharmacy closer to the nearby public road so it would benefit from public foot traffic and visibility.

The pharmacy served three main purposes. The first was the reason Moses headed that way: to care for the church members, NEATS students, and visiting pastors and missionaries. The second was to bless the community with access to medicine. (David's dream was for these pharmacies to become clinics, but you had to start somewhere. One could solve many medical problems with just a pharmacy.) The third was to have a revenue stream for ministry work. The NEATS students had a set credit amount they could use each semester.

David had to cap the students' use of the pharmacy after the first group of Darfurians came to NEATS. He learned that they would go to the local clinic for any issue, regardless of how minor. They would return and hand him their bill. David also empowered the pharmacists to give away a certain amount of medicine each month to widows and the extremely poor. Otherwise, customers had to pay, and David implored the pharmacists to run this pharmacy in the black each month.

Moses walked inside the small concrete building. He waited in a short line behind two women and an older man. When he approached the counter, he showed his student ID.

"Greetings, this morning. May I have a treatment of Coartem?" Coartem was the most popular malaria antidote for this area.

"Do you have malaria?" the young pharmacist asked Moses. Moses admired how sharp the pharmacist looked in his crisp white lab coat. Moses also noted the embroidered logo on the chest that David Kaya had custom designed.

"No, it is not me. Another student who sleeps near me. He has fever, shivering, his eyes are red. I told him I would come here to help him."

The pharmacist wrote on the box the number one and drew the sun, then he drew another numeral one and drew the moon. He told Moses, "Tell him to take one in the morning and another at night. With food is better, and finish this entire box. If he feels better, do not save the pills. Complete the box. And when he is feeling better, please tell him to come and see me. What is this student's name? I need to charge his account and not yours, unless you are sponsoring him too?"

"Abraham Maker. I cannot sponsor him today. Thank you very much for this help," Moses replied.

Moses fast-walked back to the dorm. With Abraham properly medicated, Moses had ten minutes to spare when he arrived back in the classroom for the 11 a.m. session.

Americans Appear

Professor Nicholas usually taught hermeneutics on Thursdays at 11, but President Mawa stood at the front of the class today. Two white Americans sat in light blue plastic chairs near the chalkboard.

Nicholas and five other faculty members took the first row of the classroom. At precisely 11 a.m., Mawa clapped his hands, everyone stood up, and this time, Wani, one of the older students, led them in singing "Jesus is Number One." It was fast-paced and easy to learn. One basically just repeated, "Jesus is number one" over and over.

Mawa then had everyone sit down. He oozed charisma. Mawa was what some would describe as wiry because, while thin, his muscles were clearly defined. He easily commanded the room, and everyone could feel the energy and passion he brought whenever he spoke.

"Precious students of NEATS. I am interrupting your class time today and for the next four days." Mawa articulated every word and seemed to lean forward when talking.

He continued, "Students, I want to give a special introduction to my two special American friends. For many of us, they do not need any introduction, but some of you are new and you do not know them yet."

It was clear to Moses that the faculty and many of the students knew the two men well. There were lots of smiles and waves.

Mawa had the two Americans stand. "On my left is Pastor Jason Snyder, and this other man is Pastor Duke Fisher."

Moses would later learn that, while seminary trained, Duke was not a full-time pastor. He was an engineer. It turned out that a lot of the American men he would meet would be called pastor if they taught at NEATS.

Mawa declared, "These men of God have taught at NEATS every year since 2009!"

The class erupted in applause.

"These next four days, we will pause our regular classes. We have asked our friends to bring a good study of the book of Daniel and to discuss how to have a healthy personal spiritual life as a pastor. We are all very excited." Turning to Duke and Jason, Mawa said, "You are most welcome!"

More applause.

Uncle O Preps Moses: Empower One Is Different

Moses was excited. It was only his second week, and he was already experiencing this fun part of NEATS: visitors coming all the way from America to teach in his classroom.

In the days before Moses arrived on campus, Onesimus had mentioned that he would learn from visiting faculty every once in a while. Curious, Moses asked, "Does NEATS have any American missionaries living at the school and teaching?"

Onesimus explained, "No, the Americans only come on short visits. There is a ministry that stands behind NEATS from America. It is both in America and Africa. It is called Empower One. They are quite serious about that first word in their name, Empower. Pastor David leads all of Africa. There are no Americans or Westerners who live in Africa with Empower One—only us, Africans. The team in America will tell us, 'We stand on the shoulders of former missionaries.' But this Empower One, they really believe that we can do the work of God here much better."

At that, Onesimus let out a little laugh, then said, "And we know that is true, nephew."

Moses wasn't actually Onesimus's nephew, but they'd grown so close they would call one another uncle and nephew.

Onesimus continued, "Our foods don't bother our stomachs. We don't mind sleeping in the bush. We know our *real* customs. And I have heard of the big money some missionaries from America need to live in our place. Nephew, we always wish for big money, but you know we can live on little. Pastor David has a partner at Empower One in America named Mike."

Moses adjusted himself in his chair, leaning in toward Onesimus.

"Mike and his team really understand this. They are a little bit different. You watch. These great teachers from America will come to NEATS. They will amaze you with their knowledge. But, nephew, when you are eating posha with them, these friends from America will eat posha with you and with their hands, just like you! They will use God's fork." With that, Onesimus let out a bigger laugh.

"They will listen to you and the local pastors. They will want to know what you really think about things. Do not fear telling them. They want to know. I have seen American seminary professors stop their lectures and spend even more than two days asking us questions and responding to our local problems. This Empower One brings different types of missionaries."

Moses smiled at the thought of Americans eating with their hands.

"With Empower One, the local leaders make the decisions in Africa. John Monychol decides his own strategy in the Upper Nile. The American office does not interfere. They care a lot about us reaching unreached people groups and starting new churches, but we get to decide how we do this. It is really a nice partnership, true partners."

Onesimus stood up and took two steps to the small plastic table nearby. He poured loose-leaf tea into a small strainer, just large enough to fit over the top of his cup. He poured hot water over the tea and strainer. Setting it aside, he scooped two large scoops of sugar, stirred, and sat down.

He continued. "Nephew, when you are in Kajo Keji, look around that compound carefully. You will be at NEATS. You will worship in a big church Pastor David calls a flagship church. This is a large church that will plant many churches like mine. That church oversees the work in the entire region. We start our churches under trees and maybe build with our local materials, grass and mud. Pastor David built the flagship church with blocks. They did a lot of evangelism, and you will see they have a big congregation. Pastor preaches giving, seriously. That flagship church does not need any money from America. The people support the pastor and even send missionaries from their giving."

Onesimus slurped his hot tea.

"Nephew, you will not have to pump water and carry a jerry can. In Kajo Keji, Pastor David drilled a nice well, very deep. They have a solar-powered pump that carries the water into a very large container. I think it may be twenty thousand liters! They have placed many distribution points for this clean water. You just turn a small handle. Pastor put one distribution point on the main road. They turn that on during the day for the local community. It is a blessing, nephew."

Moses took his turn and stood and walked to the table with the tea. Like Onesimus, he placed the tea leaves in the strainer and poured the water. Only he stopped halfway. He picked up a different thermos. He took the cork out of its top and poured hot milk into his cup. He scooped three large scoops of sugar into his cup and returned to his chair.

Onesimus said, "I'm telling you, one place you will be jealous, nephew, is the primary school, and the secondary school, and even the nursery school. Pastor David says, 'We must reach the next generation in South Sudan and Sudan.' You will wish you had been in these schools. Nice uniforms, nephew, very clean. The teachers are all believers, and these children get a great education, and you, as a NEATS student, will be teaching and discipling them. David says a president of South Sudan will come from our school one day."

Moses noticed a stray dog eyeing the table. Dogs here were docile from how they were treated. It kept a safe distance. It never knew when a small human might throw a rock its way.

Onesimus continued, "If you become sick, there is a pharmacy that also serves the local community, and Pastor David has a radio station. This station is very good, nephew. David has this station preaching, teaching, and discipling the entire county from its big tower."

Moses was glued to Onesimus the entire time he spoke. It made Moses even more excited, and honored, to join this work. Moses said, "Uncle, this is so great. Thank you for helping me go to NEATS and see all these wonderful things."

Onesimus replied, "It is very wonderful, nephew. And you will not be alone. Pastor David and Empower One are working on fourteen more places to put all these things. The flagship church, schools, and all these parts. They are building eleven in South Sudan. Every state will have one. Three in Sudan to reach the unreached and Muslim populations, and one in Congo."

Moses asked, "Why Congo, Uncle?"

"In 2010, three men from DR Congo came to NEATS like you. They were very quiet and kept to themselves. I think their English was not so good. But, nephew, if you meet them, listen to them and show them respect. They went back to Congo and have done a big work. Planting many churches, starting a Bible school like NEATS, and they are sending missionaries to the Pygmies in the forest. Pastor David believes they will do even greater work with their flagship church."

"Uncle, I want to meet these men from Congo. I would like to see the Pygmies."

"You will see many things, nephew. God will do many things with you."

American Teachers Who Listen Before They Teach

After Mawa introduced Jason and Duke, the entire classroom clapped their hands in unison, first slowly, then gradually faster until Jason stood in front of the class and general applause took over. Jason shook his head and put both hands up signaling the fuss and pomp embarrassed him.

"Greetings from the church in America," Jason began. "My name is Jason. I'm a pastor in America. For those who don't know me, I'm the husband of one wife, and I have two wonderful daughters."

The class broke out in applause. Moses smiled because he was witnessing how Jason was experienced in Africa. He greeted the class just like Moses would have if their roles were reversed.

Jason continued, "President Mawa has asked us to teach on the book of Daniel this week. Duke and I are excited to teach this book. But before we talk about Daniel, Duke and I want to hear about you men. And I see you ladies here. Wow! Last year, there were only three ladies in the class and now I count, what, fifteen? One third of the class. Soon you might take over." Jason laughed.

"We want to hear from all of you. We'd like to take this first bit of time and hear who you are, where you're from, and what challenges you're facing at your churches."

Moses thought, *This is exactly what Onesimus said would happen!*

Moses was prepared to only hear a lecture and take good notes. But for the rest of that day, no one talked about the prophet Daniel. Jason and Duke pivoted to help coach pastors in difficult marriages or who were having problems with troublesome deacons. They also gave advice about wayward children or churches whose people didn't give financially. He saw Duke with his hands on a pastor's shoulders at lunch, praying over him after listening intently to him.

At the dinner break, Moses found a few other Kukus. In their language and while dipping his hand in fish stew with posha, he said, "I did not expect these teachers from America to teach like this today. We spent most of today only discussing local issues." Moses laughed. "I didn't learn much about Daniel, but I learned so many things today!"

Wani had been at, or around NEATS, for three years. He told Moses, "You are at a different type of school. Number one, you will really know how to start and lead a church. These guys teaching you care a lot about pastors, church planters, and everyone here who leads any type of church. Number two, they love you. These Americans who come over will show you a lot of love. Be grateful, young man. I am telling you, be grateful."

Moses looked into his green plastic bowl with one last bite of fish and told God he was indeed grateful.

When Moses reached his bunk, Abraham was sitting up, sipping water from blue plastic coffee cup. "Shukran, my Kuku friend." Abraham said. "You were right about those pills. I am feeling stronger already. Please don't tell my mother." And they both laughed.

FRIDAY

THIS IS WHY
I AM HERE

MOSES FELT GUILTY during chapel.

He told himself, *I should feel honored to lead the devotionals at Ebenezer Academy's primary and secondary schools. But I would rather hear Duke and Jason teaching.*

He remembered in his last discipleship time that Emma had told the small group, "Good leaders sacrifice what they want for the good of those they serve."

When chapel ended, Moses walked by the kitchen on his way to the secondary school on the other side of the church compound and thought, *I can only control myself. I must have a better attitude. Take every thought captive to obey Christ. Second Corinthians 10:5.*

Mary had the ladies laughing as usual, and they all waved and greeted him. That lifted his spirits. Then, as if a small reward for obedience, Mary waved him over and handed him a piece of fried bread. He quickly found the sugar bowl, dipped the bread, and let it linger in his mouth as he continued his walk. He crossed through the famous three trees under which NEATS had begun. Today, a worker had set up sawhorses under the trees. Pastor David hired the carpenter anytime he needed a carpentry project completed at the compound. He was David's neighbor. Moses thought they had lived near one another in the refugee camps as well. The carpenter was cutting boards for rafters for the coming dining hall. Moses looked forward to eating indoors.

Through the trees, Moses crossed one corner of the football pitch. It was empty this morning except for two women crossing the other side with jerry cans of water on their heads. They reminded him of his mother.

A few more steps and he reached the assembled secondary students, all 105 of them, grades Senior One to Senior Four. They spanned from fourteen years old all the way to one student who was twenty-six and in Senior Three, but most of the oldest students were eighteen. Moses thought it odd that all the Empower One missionaries were from America because so many of the things he did in South Sudan were based on the British system, from the English words they used to their school system. He thought, *I like our numbered system better. The Americans seem to have names for each grade—freshman, something that begins with an s, and junior.* He couldn't recall the others.

He thought the students looked sharp. Each wore a crisp white shirt with the Ebenezer crest on the left breast pocket. When Pastor David started the first school in Kajo Keji, he, along with local church elders, had just studied the book of First Samuel. They recalled 1 Samuel 7:12: "Then Samuel took a stone and set it up between Mizpah and Shen and called its name Ebenezer; for he said, 'Till now the Lord has helped us.'"

Both boys and girls wore bright red ties. The boys wore gray shorts. The girls wore gray skirts that went just below their knees. They all stood in lines near the flagpole. They'd just recited their pledge to South Sudan. Moses quickly stopped and bowed his head while a Senior Four student prayed for her class and their day.

After the opening day prayer, the students turned and began walking to a smaller church building that stood about forty meters away—the original flagship church. It was much smaller than the large new one on the other end of the property.

At the sight of this smaller church, Moses remembered his first day at NEATS.

The Flagship Church Origin Story

The real Professor Nicholas teaching at NEATS in 2014.

Professor Nicholas had led him and the other new students through an orientation. He had them stand under a group of trees beside the church so the sun wouldn't beat down on their heads. Kajo Keji is only six degrees north of the equator, and the daytime sun can feel intense.

While they observed the church, Nicholas explained, "Th-th-this church is what launched the flagship church vision. Students, from here is what is now driving almost everything Pastor David does these days." (No one ever mentioned his stutter, nor did it seem to bother anyone.)

He continued, "P-P-Pastor David, Edward Dima, and Kenneth Duku were all living in a refugee camp in northern Uganda in the 1990s. Our civil war in Sudan that started in 1983 was still going on during this time. A missionary from America, K-K-Kentucky, named Harold Cathey showed up at their camp. Harold Cathey spent time observing them and getting to know them. Pastor Cathey invited them to study at G-G-Global Theological Seminary in Jinja, Uganda. They were excited, and they went to GTS immediately."

Moses would come to learn that Professor Nicholas was the longest-serving faculty member, that he'd been there from the beginning with Edward Dima under three trees by the football pitch. Everyone deeply respected him.

Nicholas paused. He looked at the group and said, "E-e-even today. You must begin learning how to be church leaders. Pastor Cathey discipled your church fathers. One day, you must do the same. Pastor Cathey had the original vision for flagship churches. He raised some small money and helped Pastor David build this flagship church in 2002, while the war was still going."

Moses studied the structure, thinking about what it must have taken to build.

Nicholas continued, "Pastor Cathey taught Pastor David that a strong flagship church would be like a hub in a wheel of church planting. He encouraged Pastor David to evangelize this entire area, grow the church, and to preach the Bible. He also encouraged Pastor David to teach biblical giving. This way the church could support itself. We can send our own missionaries out. And we will not depend on America or anyone else. After the opening dedication of this first flagship church, Pastor Cathey told David, 'Now God will care for you.' He was aging, and he had to go back to K-Kentucky."

A pang shot in Moses's gut. He had a fleeting thought of his father. He never knew when these pangs would occur. But as he imagined Pastor Cathey leaving Pastor David, he suddenly wanted to see his father.

Nicholas said, "We had a great time from 2006 until 2016, when the war came here and pushed us back into the camps. In that time, this flagship church planted sixty-seven churches in just this area around here. You, Moses, your home church with Onesimus is one of those churches. Your pastor worshiped here and learned here just like you are now."

Moses gave a weak smile. Nicholas invoking Onesimus's name made him think once more of his father. In that moment he felt the hole his father's absence left inside of him. A sadness covered him. Onesimus, his uncle, and James, the deacon at his church, both were like fathers to him. But it wasn't the same. Despite his father abandoning him and his mother, he still longed to be with his father. To walk along the footpaths with him. To hunt with him like other boys did with their fathers. To sit by the fire at night and hear his father tell stories and give him advice.

"In this last exile, we leaders realized what we had here was special." Nicholas shook him out of his reverie. Nicholas paused, then said, "This place was a great incubator for church planters and leaders. Students like you would come to this church and watch Pastors Edward, David, and Kenneth lead a big church. We taught them the Bible and theology at NEATS. We had the students do outreaches, disciple new believers, and plant new churches in the villages. Almost all the best leaders at Empower One today came from this time period here in Kajo Keji. You are next, students, now that we are back again with this new peace."

Moses thought, *This is exactly why I am here. If I can start good churches, more fathers will find Jesus and love their families properly.*

Just then Nicholas finished with, "This is why I am here. We must see this vision become real."

Teaching and Preaching: At NEATS, You Learn and Do

Moses snapped back to his assignment at Ebenezer Chapel.

He looked away from that grove of trees to the side door of the church. He walked up the small staircase inside the church, which was just one large sanctuary with concrete block walls covered with plaster, a tiled floor, wooden rafters with lights strung through them, and a metal roof. He was glad it wasn't raining. Otherwise, it would be impossible for the students to hear him, even with the sound system they ran using the solar energy powering the entire property.

Moses walked up another small set of stairs and approached the pulpit. On the right side of the church, the secondary students took seats in plastic chairs. On the left, over two hundred primary students crammed in. They were free to sit where they liked among the lines of plastic chairs, but on both sides, boys sat with boys and girls with girls. The bright red ties on the white shirts popped throughout the sanctuary.

Moses suddenly felt nervous. These were just kids, but this was the largest group he'd ever spoken in front of. Emma had reviewed Moses's lesson and offered coaching tips. "Moses, my young friend, teaching at Ebenezer Chapel is part of being at NEATS. Here, you don't just learn in the classroom. Here, at NEATS, you *do*. You do things. Even one day, you may preach at the flagship church. But today we are starting you at Ebenezer Chapel. These are the future leaders of South Sudan. Take care, my friend. Bring God's word to these young people. The future president of our country may be in one of these classes."

When Emma slid in the back door and took a seat behind the secondary students, Moses's nerves increased. He knew Emma would have much preferred to listen to Jason and Duke. Yet again, his mentor was modeling how to disciple.

After praying and calling for two worship songs, Moses had all the students sit down. He nervously opened his Bible to James 2, read the entire chapter, then he stepped from behind the pulpit and began to teach—and even preach a little.

"Students, if the local commissioner comes to our church, do we show him honor? Yes, of course, but does God want us to show the commissioner more honor than the drunkard who comes to our church looking for Jesus? No, we are all created in God's image, and we are all equal in God's eyes. God has a heart for the poor and the suffering. God will use that commissioner, but he calls us to love that drunkard and to welcome him as well."

He liked to move as he spoke. Once he felt that he was connecting with the students—meeting their eyes, seeing them actually listen—he felt great.

The Constructive Critique

Moses noted the carpenter's progress in the little time he had been teaching when he walked back to the NEATS portion of the compound. He stopped at the kitchen and poured himself a cup of tea; he had that special feeling again. The same feeling he had when helping his mother and the pastors at his home church. He felt like God saw him and was pleased with him. Like he was on the right track and was doing what God had made him for. He found a weak but recovering Abraham who asked, "How was it, Moses?"

"So good, brother. I was nervous when I stood at the pulpit. Even singing, which you know I love, was difficult for me this morning. And Emma came to watch me and listen."

"What did Emma say to you after?"

"He is a good teacher. He told me I was moving a bit too much. He said a little is fine, but I was walking too much. He told me to make my explanation of faith and works a little more simple for the younger students. But he said I did good and he could see me preaching in the flagship church one Sunday." Moses revealed a big smile.

Moses closed his eyes and whispered his thanks to God, not only for the tea but also for God bringing him to this place. Then it was time to grab a notebook and learn about the book of Daniel from Duke.

SATURDAY

A MOVIE IN A VILLAGE

Jesus Film showing in a refugee camp in northern Uganda.

It was only Moses's second Saturday as a NEATS student, but today would not follow the normal schedule. Moses suspected it was for

Duke and Jason's comfort. The faculty had arranged for a later start time this morning. He had no idea what jet lag meant, but he saw fatigue on their faces when the room got too warm in the afternoon.

Typically, no classes were held on Saturdays, except language instruction for the Darfurians. They'd spend four hours with their English tutor on Saturdays. Today, Mawa had instructed the students to be in the classroom at 9:30 a.m. "My dears, welcome to this special Saturday teaching at NEATS. Yesterday was so wonderful. Thank you, Pastors Jason and Duke, for caring about us so much. Today's program will look like this: Five-minute break at 11:15 a.m. Five minutes only. Break for lunch at 1 p.m. sharp, and you are to return to these seats at 2:15 p.m. sharp. We will conclude at 4:30 p.m. for the Jesus Film mission tonight. Pastor Duke will begin our teaching in the book of Daniel. Moses, you come to the front and lead us in singing, then Pastor Duke, you are most welcome."

After the singing, Duke rose and walked to the front of the classroom and said, "Please open your Bibles to the book of Daniel."

Moses had never looked at Daniel with the depth he was learning today. But beyond that, he was amazed at how Daniel connected to other books in the Bible. *Aha! This is a big reason Jesus referred to himself as Son of Man*, he thought as Duke taught. He had tripped over that in Mark chapter 8, but now the dots connected. He had briefly learned about the Roman Empire in school, but he had not heard of Alexander the Great. *The Bible impacts history*, he thought, and he was amazed at scripture from a Jewish man writing hundreds of years before Jesus's birth and while in exile. As a South Sudanese, Moses felt a tiny kinship with Daniel as someone who'd experienced exile firsthand. He couldn't write fast enough in the class to capture not only what Duke was teaching but also where his mind was leading him. He had moments where he felt he was reading the Bible for the first time all over again.

When the class broke for the day, Moses was filled with conflicting feelings again. A part of him wanted to change into his T-shirt and slides, sit with his brothers, and talk about what they were learning about the Bible. Those downtimes were so rich for him. Beyond Onesimus and two deacons, he hadn't had many long conversations about certain verses or passages. He had an understanding of doctrine as a concept, but until now he'd never really discussed it or even remotely thought of why you should have it and apply it.

Today's downtime conversation would have to wait. Tonight, he was going out in the big truck again. This time, it was to play the Jesus Film in a nearby village. He had never seen the movie, but the older students said it was a great experience.

Professor Andrew would be their chaperone again. He was drinking tea with mechanic extraordinaire and driver, Lagu, by Seed Effect's office. Their office sat beside Empower One's on the compound. Moses looked forward to learning more about Seed Effect. During the orientation, Nicholas had Fiona, Seed Effect's Africa director, tell the new students about Seed Effect. "Welcome new students of NEATS." She began that day with a smooth Ugandan accent. Moses was impressed that a young woman led such a big organization.

Fiona said, "Seed Effect began here in Kajo Keji many years ago. We started as a microfinance ministry. When the war came, we changed to become a savings group ministry. We mostly serve refugees in the camps in northern Uganda, but we recently moved back home to Kajo Keji. We are very happy that we have one hundred thousand people in our savings groups. And they are almost all refugees."

The students applauded when they heard that number.

She continued, "We empower the local people to save their small money. They lend this money to members of their groups to improve their businesses. When they repay these loans, the group benefits from the interest rate. The groups each decide their own rate as well. We do not dictate these rates. You students, we are glad you are here. Many of you will be pastors. Our groups are good for your churches because, as the people grow economically, they can support the church. We love our groups near your churches because many people find Jesus in our groups, and we need your help discipling them."

Moses didn't know what an interest rate was, but he couldn't wait to tell his mother about Seed Effect and that they were back in South Sudan. She would love to be in a Seed Effect group. She only sold vegetables now, but he recalled her reluctantly telling him, "You know, Moses, I was good at business when I was selling sorghum wine. I watched the other women not take care with their measurements. Many took too much credit. Not me. I did not allow anyone to buy on credit. I even knew to keep some *sim sim* seeds in bags because my customers would want a small snack."

He had made a mental note to try to connect his mother to Seed Effect when he saw her on his next break in two months.

Wani got Moses's attention. They each took one side of a large speaker and loaded it into the lorry. With thirty of the students coming in the lorry, they made light work of loading the speakers, generator, table, chairs, specially cut bamboo poles, and a large backpack.

Andrew gathered the students. Tonight, they would show the Jesus Film at a church in Litoba, another village about thirty minutes away by lorry.

Lights, Movie, Action: 1970s Jesus Wows the Village!

When they arrived, Moses followed Wani and Julius, another older student. He had never experienced this before, so he fell in with the guys who'd set up over a dozen of these showings. Denis, the Litoba church's pastor, pointed to an open field. Moses noted the freshly cut grass around the edge of the opening. Denis's church had cleared and cleaned the area for this night.

Wani drove the bamboo poles into the ground, tied a crossbar at the top, and tied the poles to stakes he drove into the ground to keep them upright. Julius stood on one of the plastic chairs. He had a large white sheet over his shoulder. Moses noticed someone had put homemade grommets on three sides of the sheet. Julius looped a plastic string someone had made by carefully pulling apart a United Nations–supplied tarp through the grommets and around the poles.

While Wani and Julius installed the screen, a group of ladies set the plastic table in place about twelve meters away from the screen. Moses was surprised at how tiny the projector was. All the cords were marked by unique colors, making it easy for the ladies to know where to plug the projector to the battery, amplifier, microphone, and speaker. They always brought the generator just in case, but tonight the battery looked strong. As far as Moses knew, in the entire area only the Catholic church and the NEATS compound had electricity, and both used solar.

Church members scurried around, placing chairs and laying mats down so people wouldn't have to sit on the grass or dirt. The lorry alone had drawn attention, and people were already checking out what was going on. Denis had sent the youth group throughout the village the past two days, inviting everyone they saw to come tonight.

Moses looked to his right and saw the church. It was more established than his home church, which met under a tree. Denis had put up a church building about fifteen feet wide by forty feet long. It had thick mud walls, with small windows cut out for airflow. Each window had a shutter that looked like a small door. It could unlatch and swing open, framed with wood and covered with metal. The metal for these windows were United States Agency for International Development (USAID) cooking oil cans, beaten flat and nailed to the frame. USAID was America's massive relief and aid organization that Moses had grown up appreciating, especially the beans and maize he'd enjoyed from their sacks. The door to the church had the same wooden frame, but it was made of corrugated metal. Denis covered the church with thick thatched grass so that it looked like a larger, rectangular tukul. The pews inside were like those found under the trees, with logs laid across two Y-shaped logs driven into the floor.

Darkness was falling. Moses looked westward and watched the sun as it set behind a few low mountains in the distance. The last twenty minutes or so of the sunset turned the sky pink and orange. It was beautiful. It made Moses miss his mom and siblings when they would talk and laugh as the sun set.

An old man carrying a carved stick interrupted Moses's trance. He stuck his hand out for Moses to shake. Moses noticed the man's face was a little wet, and he could smell the soap from his clean skin. This *musei*, what one called an older man, had taken a quick bucket bath for the big event. Moses shook his hand.

Then Moses heard Wani tap on the microphone, breathe into it three or four times, and begin to sing. The event was starting.

The students, women's group, and church members immediately began clapping, dancing, and singing. Two teenage boys looked at one another and took off running. They quickly returned with a large goatskin drum and took turns keeping the beat. Two of the female church members had homemade tambourines, made from beating flat two USAID metal cooking oil cans. They'd put the two pieces together, placed small stones inside, and crimped the edges so it formed what looked like a large envelope. As they sang and danced, they shook the stones.

Everyone sang, drummed, or danced for an hour. Moses gladly thought, *We're not in the rigorous time constraints of NEATS now.*

Moses kept seeing flashlights bobbing toward them from every direction. The crowd, now sitting in a circle around the screen, easily numbered in the hundreds. Wani signaled for the singing to stop. "Greetings, my friends in Litoba! Tonight, we have brought you something very special. Together, we will watch a true story from the Bible. This is God's word to us."

Wani held a Bible high above his head. "Everything you see and hear in this movie really happened and is true. I want to appreciate Pastor Denis, who I think most of you know. That is his church there." Wani pointed toward the mud-walled church. "I also want to recognize our leader, Pastor and Professor Andrew Yunda from NEATS Bible School in Wudu."

Everyone politely applauded.

Wani waved his hand in the direction of the NEATS students. "All of us will remain here after the movie to pray for anyone and to discuss anything you see in this film."

With that, the movie, made in 1979 by Campus Crusade for Christ (now called Cru) kicked off.

Moses was glad he stood near the back of the crowd. The seats close to the screen were good, but the light drew a lot of bugs. No one seemed to mind. The crowd was mesmerized. It became an interactive experience. When Jesus restored the sight of the blind man, the crowd erupted into cheers. When the soldier nailed Jesus to the cross, women began to wail and cry.

When the movie ended, Wani took the microphone. "My dear beloved in Litoba, do you see how much God loves you? Jesus Christ, who sat on a throne in heaven, came here to die for you and me. Jesus has brought the kingdom of God to all of us. God wants you to live in his kingdom, with him, even while we live here in Litoba."

The speakers suddenly buzzed and crackled, causing Wani to move farther from them.

Moses heard Wani walk them through the part he was more familiar with and knew was essential: They, like Wani, did bad things and fell short of God's glory, and only Jesus could take away their sins.

Wani said, "But, my friends, Jesus came to rescue us from our sin, not condemn you. He has come to give you everlasting life."

It was Wani's heartfelt description of Jesus coming to rescue them and invite them into his kingdom and live life with him that put a lump in Moses's throat.

Moses felt a warmth from how Wani spoke that night, as if he could peer inside the minds of those gathered around him.

"I know you are tired inside," Wani continued. "Always worrying if you have angered your ancestors. Did you make the right sacrifice to your family's spirits? Or to this village's spirits?"

Many in the crowd moved uncomfortably.

"Let us end these worries tonight. The same God who created all the stars we are seeing, even tonight when we look up, loves you and wants you to never worry again."

More dots were connecting in Moses's mind. He thought of his mother. *Jesus had set her free. Free from feeling overlooked and abandoned as a third wife, free from distilling moonshine to medicate others' trauma, free from feelings of hopelessness.* Today she sang, laughed, and held her family together.

Moses felt like there was another wonderful part of the gospel invading his heart and mind that night. He had accepted his sinfulness and his need for God to cleanse him, but this concept of now walking with Jesus in his kingdom, even in South Sudan, filled him with a renewed joy.

Wani continued, "My friends, Jesus is still alive from his resurrection. He can hear you even now. You call to him. Or, you come. You are free to come. Someone here can pray for you, talk with you, help you."

That was Moses's cue. Along with his fellow students, ladies, and Denis's church members, Moses headed to the lorry to be available to talk about Jesus. Moses turned around from the lorry and thought there had been a misunderstanding: Almost the entire crowd was lining up. He felt like he was dreaming.

Without hesitation, the first woman asked him, "What must I do to be saved?"

He prayed with young and old, men and women. Some looked stoic and others cried. Some just wanted prayer for a sickness, some for school fees, and a few for food. He made sure Denis knew who was going hungry. The church would bring those families food.

Andrew felt God's Spirit and power that night. He didn't push. He waited, talking and praying with many of the people in the community as well. It was just after midnight when he knew it was okay to leave.

"Wani!" Andrew boomed.

The crowd quieted.

Andrew said, "Give God thanks for his night. And students. You be sure to record everything for Pastor Denis." Follow-up was critical.

Wani prayed over everyone remaining.

It was 2 a.m. when Moses stretched out on his real bed with a real pillow and a sheet to cover himself. "Thank you, King Jesus, for this bed."

Suddenly he felt overcome with emotion. Tears welled in his eyes, but he wasn't sad. He was . . . what? Happy? Yes, but that wasn't quite right. Joy. That's what he was feeling, joy. His heart was so full of joy, yet he felt conflicted because part of him didn't feel like he deserved to feel so good. He'd experienced the power of God, in person, and he'd gotten to be a part of it. Two weeks in as a student and future church planter. This would be his life.

"Oh Lord, thank you."

It felt so inadequate. It was so much deeper than that. He had experienced salvation. He loved God, but tonight Moses felt God's kingdom. He was in it and now he knew it.

"Oh Lord, thank you," he whispered over and over until he drifted to sleep.

PART 2

FLAWED PEOPLE ARE GOD'S SPECIALTY

MY STORY

San Antonio, Texas, USA, December 1999

I **WAS LOOKING DIRECTLY** into a mirror, and I didn't recognize the face in it.

It was 2 a.m. in a hotel on the Riverwalk in San Antonio. I was there for work at what is now AT&T. I was as far from God as I had ever been. Everyone's bottom is different. I had just found mine. Who had I become?

I was a poor fit inside a giant company. I felt like my soul was dying. I wasn't particularly good at the core parts of a telecom business, and I was defeated by observing people manage their careers instead of the business. The vanity and vapidness of corporate politics was, well, vain and vapid. One of my bosses asked me, "Do you know what we do around here, Mike? We push Jello. We push and think we've made a dent, and then it just pops back to its original shape."

How about that to get you out of bed in the morning? But he was right. At my level in the corporation, which was low, I was a tiny part inside of a gear within a gear, within a giant machine. "Meaningless, meaningless . . ." (Eccl. 1:1–3). Solomon was right.

I wanted to start my own business, but every time I moved in that direction, I felt like God said no. Or maybe I was too scared. Or both? I sustained myself by telling myself there was nobility in providing for my family. But every week I had the Sunday night blues and was growing in misery.

My hotel mirror experience was in December 1999. I stayed in that state of acute pain until May of 2000. In that five-month period, I felt as if all the color had gone out in the world. I tried to crawl through the day: get to lunch, get home, get to dinner, get to bed. Repeat.

In May, I decided I'd had enough and needed to go to God.

I was sitting in my office, wrestling with God. I had the gospel wrong. My wrestling was consumed with me thinking about the things I needed to give up. I didn't want to give things up. In some cases, I didn't think I could.

But that is not how God or the gospel works. It's not about regulating behavior. Those were the chains I would "see" on believers later. But whether it's the prodigal son (Luke 15), the tax collector beating his chest (Luke 18), or Mary Magdalene (Luke 8), God just wants us to come to him with our brokenness.

So that's what I did.

I got out of my chair and walked over to a conference room no one used.

I went inside, got on my knees, and surrendered, fully, to God.

In that cold, sterile, gray conference room, I prayed two prayers.

"Father, I'm done. I can't do this anymore. I'll do anything you tell me to do." I prayed, literally from my knees. "I'll go anywhere you tell me to go, I'll stand on my head, I'll do anything. I'm yours."

Then I paused and prayed, "Lord, I'm sorry to ask this, but would you please show me some fun, cool Christians because I don't see or know any around me."

I realize now that the second prayer revealed my immaturity, but it was honest and where I was at. God is so good and gentle. He meets us where we're at. He is always available in any state we find ourselves. If you invite him in and try to follow him with all your heart, he meets you there. Then, if you stick with him, he brings you into his kingdom while on earth and gives you the adventure of a lifetime, tailored uniquely to you.

What Are You Passionate About?

From that moment of surrender, I pursued God and built and rebuilt my relationship with him. I wanted to start my own business. My Sunday school teacher at the time, Reed, owned a successful wholesale insurance brokerage. He knew I was interested in becoming an entrepreneur, so he invited me to breakfast and said, "You can ask me anything you want, and I'll see if I can help you."

I slid into the booth at Denny's, and we started talking.

After a bit, Reed paused, looked up, and asked me, "Mike, what are you passionate about?"

I can still vividly recall how I felt when he asked that simple question: I couldn't think of anything. Not even something like cars or video games. Nothing. I had this pathetic thought pop in my mind that I liked to go camping, but it didn't rise to passion. It was a horrible feeling. It confirmed to me that I was a passionless drone at a giant company. I'd become my worst nightmare.

After I stumbled around mumbling, Reed suggested, "I want you to write a personal mission statement. Write it out, then let's go to breakfast again and talk about it."

Coming from anyone else, I would have dismissed the idea as cheesy. But a disciple or mentee does what his mentor suggests. The problem was, I had no idea what a personal mission statement was. I

Googled it. Essentially, it was one paragraph that stated what I wanted my life to be about. My noncompromisable values for me, my family, and my vocation.

It was a great piece of advice.

I crafted my mission statement, printed it out, and I kept it in my drawer at work. I've subsequently lost it, but I know I wanted my life to count for God. To join him in doing something far larger than me, and I wanted an adventure. I also recall I wanted to not only provide for my family but also be an example to my kids of someone who took a leap of faith. It became my touchstone, the filter I'd use to decide what I wanted to do. And it was about to come in handy.

ROUTED TO BEIRUT

I N 2003, MY wife, Ali, and I saw in the church bulletin an invitation to go to Lebanon with our pastor and his wife. We had developed a love of travel, and I thought going to Beirut sounded like a cool adventure. Plus, I love their food. This was my honest motivation for my first-ever international mission trip: adventure and food.

I said I was pursuing God, not that I'd arrived.

I pointed at the trip in the bulletin, showing Ali.

When we got home, we talked more about it. Ali said, "Well, my bonus is pretty much exactly what it would cost for us to go."

We went to the information meeting about the trip. There was Mac, our pastor, and his wife, Debbie. Also in the room were a professor from Criswell College, the president of the Baptist Convention of Texas, a seminary student, a seminary graduate, a couple, a single young lady who'd gone on countless short-term mission trips, Don Knobler (who'd taught in a seminary in Eastern Europe)—and us.

On the trip application that night, I wrote at the bottom, "I think I'm the spiritual weak link on this team." Ali had been volunteering for evangelism outreach programs. I had not. I had nothing, but Beirut sounded awesome, I was pursuing God, and I loved Lebanese food.

How about that for a deeply spiritual missional calling?

Ali was four months pregnant with our son, and her doctor told her not to go. Was it because he was concerned about Lebanon or because he was a Mormon? We didn't know, and we decided to take the risk and go.

Beirut used to be called the Paris of the Middle East. We saw evidence of that on our trip: The French-inspired architecture, the fashion of the people, and wide boulevards. We also saw bombed out buildings and evidence of war. It was intoxicating for me.

An Inspiring Eccentric

Once in Beirut, Ali and I gravitated to Don Knobler and spent quite a bit of time with him. I felt like he was part of the answer to my prayer for fun, cool Christians. He was the best kind of nutty. I had been aware of who he was because he sat courtside at Dallas Mavericks games, and the TV cameras picked up on him. He was the Mavericks' version of the eccentric Jimmy Goldstein, famous for sitting courtside at countless LA Clippers and NBA Finals games.

Don unironically wore cowskin clogs on the trip, got a kick out of greeting people with an Arabic phrase that sounded like an English curse word, and was just a lot of fun. They told him before the trip to tone down what he normally wears because it was too ostentatious for a mission trip. At the time, he was the number two Versace customer in Dallas. He loved Jesus and was living full blast.

We gathered in a room for instructions. A local missionary started, "I have some bad news. We had translators for you, but they backed out at the last minute."

Oooookay.

He continued, "We have a neighborhood mapped out for you. We're going to give you satchels that we've packed with Arabic New Testaments. Since you don't have translators, we're going to teach you a few Arabic phrases. One is 'We have a free gift for you.' Then you can hand them a New Testament and that may lead to a gospel conversation. We also have EvangeCubes for you to use as well." To understand what an EvangeCube is, think Rubik's Cube, but instead it unfolds to tell the story of the gospel of Jesus.

I was nervous but willing.

They divided us into teams. My team consisted of Ali, who could pass for Lebanese looks-wise, and Penny, who couldn't. Penny was quite blonde. My team was the only team with only one male: me.

God was arranging things.

As the only guy on our team, it forced me into the lead. If we ran into local men, they would only talk to me.

We ran into a lot of local men.

On the second day going out, where our first goal was to get past high-rise doormen in a wealthy, Muslim Beirut neighborhood, a group of young men approached us. They weren't necessarily menacing, but they didn't look friendly. What we were doing was probably not okay, and it was just me and the two ladies.

When they got to within roughly three feet of us, Ali, out of nervousness, belted out, "Jesus!" No hello, no avoidance, just "Jesus!"

Before I could even mentally fire away a *What on earth are you doing?!*, the lead guy's entire countenance changed.

He smiled and asked what we were doing. After listening, he gave us his approval, and in a courtyard where many could see us, he kissed me on both cheeks.

When he and his group turned and walked away, I read on all their backs a stitched sign: "Security." They were the local security force for that entire block of buildings. We had just been publicly given the green light by the locals.

Isn't God fun?

Wait, You're Who?

On another day, a young man approached us. He introduced us to a middle-aged man who looked so stereotypically Muslim that he could have been straight out of central casting. He had a beard and a bruised forehead, which indicated a serious Muslim who prays five times each day. He wore a *thobe*, the flowing outfit you see Middle Eastern men wear. His entire thobe was white. He covered his head with a *taqiyah*, or a form-fitting skull cap. He asked us to follow him into a building. Like idiots, we blindly followed him through hallways and corridors until we came to his office. We took seats in front of his desk across from him.

Penny extended her hand for a greeting and handshake. It hung in the air awkwardly. She forgot that a serious Muslim man would not even address her, much less touch her.

He totally ignored her. His English wasn't great, but he asked us, "What is your mission? Who sent you? Why are you here?"

I tried to politely evade his questions.

He continued, pounding his index finger on his desk as he asked, "Where are you staying? What is the name of your hotel? Did the Jews send you?"

The girls sat silent.

I kept evading and tried to read the situation.

A fifteen-year-old boy appeared in the doorway. Because the gentlemen asking questions had only rudimentary English, I looked at the boy and asked, "Do you speak English?"

"Yes, I do," said the teenager.

I put my hand into my satchel with the Arabic New Testaments and an EvangeCube. I held onto the EvangeCube.

The middle-aged man kept repeating his question. "What is your mission?"

Okay, here we go, I thought. I pulled out the EvangeCube and, with the help of my new translator, walked him through the gospel. At the end, I asked the man, "Would you like to follow Jesus?"

He leaned back. The intimidation and menace left his face. He said no, but he said it gently. He took out an ID card, slightly larger than our driver's licenses in America. He slid it across the desk to me.

It seemed odd, but I read it: *Grand Mufti* _____ .

Goodness gracious.

I had just shared the gospel and talked about the New Testament to one of the highest-ranking Muslims in Beirut. (I'm not disclosing his name for the sake of his privacy.)

I could not believe the surreal situation I'd found myself in. The spiritual weak link on the team got to tell one of the top Muslims about Jesus. And I only did so because our translators had backed out at the last minute and my team was the only one without another male.

Funny how God works. He meets us where we are.

I asked the mufti, "Would you like a local Arabic speaker to talk more about this with you?

He wrote down his email and gave it to me.

I have no idea what became of him, but I'm hopeful.

That's My Dream Job

On the last night of the trip, we had a team dinner. One of the guys on the trip grew up a Muslim, was a seminary graduate, and was working at Kroger, a grocery store. We'll call him E because he's still active in the field.

Pastor Mac was listening to E's story. Then Mac looked at E and said, full of exasperation, "What are you doing working at Kroger?! You need to come work for the church. Listen, E, I need someone who can help us focus on four places in the world for our mission's emphasis. I need you to build a strategy for each area. And I want you to mobilize our people to participate in those missions."

I leaned over to Ali and said, "That's my dream job, but I don't want to go to seminary, and I don't want to work at a local church."

Ali filed that away.

THE LEAP

SOON THEREAFTER, WHILE sitting at our dining room table, Ali told me, "You need to meet Woodlyn's husband, Mike. He works for an organization with a lot of ex-professionals like you."

Woodlyn Jorgensen had been mentoring Ali in a young mothers' program at our church. Years earlier, Mike had left practicing law to join a ministry called e3 Partners. They were a church-planting ministry working all over the world, but the Americans on staff lived in America and traveled back and forth internationally. I'd later learn that was termed a nonresidential ministry model. God had absolutely wrecked Mike. He'd laid on his bedroom floor facedown, weeping because God was all over him. He'd given up his partnership, raised support, and joined e3 Partners.

We went to lunch with Mike and Woodlyn, and Mike talked to me about the ministry. It sounded great. Then he mentioned that all the staff raised their support. That means each staff member had to personally fundraise his or her total salary.

I thought, *That sounds great, but no thanks on the support thing.* I didn't tell him that then because I didn't want to begin a conversation that would lead to me telling him I wasn't interested in joining e3. That's how I felt: *Sounds like he found his place, but I'll keep looking.* I was glad to have met Mike, but I thought that was the end of that relationship.

However, Mike pursued me and a couple months later invited me to come on a short-term mission trip with him to Bolivia. He said, "But don't write a check for this trip. I want you to send out support letters for your trip."

I think I just passively agreed. On the inside, that was the last thing I wanted to do. I don't know if I could have named the two forces swirling inside of me when he made that suggestion. But I can now: pride and insecurity. *What would people think if I asked them for support for my trip? Would I be broadcasting that I wasn't professionally successful?*

But I respected Mike. If a guy who'd left a prestigious law firm could do it, so could I. I swallowed my pride and mailed eighty letters asking for help to go to Bolivia.

Thirty-two people responded.

They gave so much that I had enough money for two trips.

God was sending me another message.

On that Bolivia trip, Mike assigned me to the home of a church deacon. The deacon had agreed to start a church in his house. We were the starting crew. He had zero church members when we arrived. At the end of that week, 110 people were worshiping in his front yard.

I felt like I was walking in the Book of Acts. I heard a few years ago that the church was still going, with about fifty to sixty members.

"You Think Money Is Hard for Me?" —God

I love folks who walk with a spiritual limp. The way I define that is they've either screwed up royally or been hurt deeply, but in either case they've come to or returned to God. They *get* mercy and grace on a deep level because they've required so much of it. Clearly, I put myself in this camp as well. Joe Balzer walked with such a limp. Joe had gotten thrown into federal prison for flying a plane drunk—kinda. (He wasn't actually doing the flying, and it's a longer story, which he tells in his book *Flying Drunk: The True Story of a Northwest Airlines Flight, Three Drunk Pilots, and One Man's Fight for Redemption*.) His gospel redemption story is powerful. So I pay attention to guys like Joe.

He listened to me process my trips to Lebanon and Bolivia. I told him that I thought perhaps God was calling me into something much bigger. Joe then handed me a book. "I think you should read this, Mike."

I looked at the cover: *Wild at Heart* by John Eldredge. As soon as I saw it, I thought, *Yes. This is what God knows I need right now.*

I started reading it that night. And God stopped me in my tracks when I read this line: "It's going to take risk, and danger, and there's the catch—are we willing to live with the level of risk God invites us to?"[1]

When I read those lines, I thought of Ali. *Who will she wake up next to in ten years? The guy who chose risk and danger or the guy who didn't?*

God uses all sorts of stuff to get our attention and motivate us.

This is the thing about calling: It's unique to you.

We want to see the burning bush or have a visit from an angel of the Lord or receive a vision. And hooray for those who receive visions when God calls them to their task.

But callings can be more mundane—if you're being attentive. Even if you're not, God can still get your attention through addition. That entire year, everything felt like it pointed me toward taking the leap into full-time missions: the movies I watched, the conversations I had, and the books I read. God just kept stacking my signs up one after another.

My last hurdle was money.

I still didn't want to raise our salary.

---

1 John Eldredge, *Wild at Heart* (Nashville: Thomas Nelson, 2001), 46.

In that same time period, I was on a small homeless ministry's board. The executive director had a big vision for a Christmas event that would cost $65,000. At the time of this vision, around September, we had negative $5,000 in our account. By the time the event occurred, we had more than enough funds.

God asked me, "Do you think money is hard for me?"

He reminded me of the one letter for Bolivia and that homeless ministry event. He also brought back to mind how, years earlier, Ali and I had trusted God when she'd abruptly quit her job to stay home with our daughter for a season.

He removed my final fear.

I'd found my passion, I was willing to take the leap, and I had a place to jump.

In January 2005, Ali and I sat at our dining room table once again. I said, "God is telling me to raise support and go full time at e3."

She said, "I've seen this coming for a year. I'm scared, but I trust God, and I trust you."

We took the leap.

THE WALL

SOMETIMES, I LIKE to poke the guys I know serving on church staffs by saying, "Everyone in ministry ought to have to raise support at least once in their life. That's how you will truly know if you're called."

It's an incredible filter. And one of the hardest things I've ever done. If you're not called, or your spouse is not one hundred percent with you, you won't make it. However, if you commit, it's a tremendous faith builder.

I enrolled and went through training with an organization that today is called Via. What a blessing because they taught me that from God's perspective, people's giving is vertical, meaning it's between them and God. That depressurized the process a bit for me. Because if someone said yes, it wasn't because I was awesome or clever. And when they said no, it wasn't a rejection of me. That helped a lot. I also felt and still feel that I am a heavenly kingdom catalyst. Anyone who invests in the ministry with us will share in God's rewards for every church started, salvation granted, and refugee fed.

Ali loved the practical teaching Via provided regarding if we could ever take a vacation again or buy a new couch. Because whether rational or not, you feel like you live in a fishbowl. You feel as if any-one supporting you is questioning your purchases and lifestyle. You think people are asking "Did Mike and Ali use my $50 per month support to buy that car? Because that seems excessive."

You start to feel guilty and self-conscious about each purchase you make. The training pointed us to Paul's words in Philippians 4:11–12: "Not that I speak from want, for I have learned to be con-tent in whatever circumstances I am. I know how to get along with humble means, and I also know how to live in prosperity; in any and every circumstance I have learned the secret of being filled and going hungry, both of having abundance and suffering need." Shoot for the middle. Care a lot about stewardship, but don't let living on support paralyze you.

The process for raising support is straightforward: Make a list of every human being you have any connection to whatsoever. Prioritize that list. Mail those folks letters. When I raised support, we mailed physical letters. Next, call and ask to meet with them. Meet, prefer-ably in person, cast vision, and ask them to join your support team at $X per month.

It was one of the most wonderful and terrible processes I've ever gone through. First, some of the terrible.

The phone felt like a thousand-pound weight. I'd sit in my home office at night and would be filled with dread. I'd have to think about Ali and the kids to force myself to make calls.

I kept my full-time job for most of the process. That meant except for Friday night, I spent every other moment of free time raising support. I essentially didn't see my family for eleven months.

I wasn't allowed to do field ministry until I hit one hundred percent of my support goal. At eighty percent, I ran out of people to talk to. They call that "the wall." I smashed into it. I had around four hundred and sixty names when I started, and I had gone through all of them. I then had to go back to the people who said yes four and five months earlier and ask them for referrals. That was brutal too.

One of my high school Sunday school teachers hung up on me when I called for an appointment.

When I eventually resigned from AT&T, I asked my boss at the time, who was a believer, if he could use me to reduce headcount. It was the fourth quarter, there were always layoffs. At first, I hoped he could lay me off and I could have a little severance. When he said no to that, I asked if he could lay me off to save someone else's job. He said no to that too. Much later, I set up a support appointment with him and his wife. Did I mention you get desperate in this process? Not only did he say no to support, but he said I lacked faith when I asked him for the layoff.

Ouch.

Finally, one of the hard things is people occasionally referring you to George Mueller. He's famous for starting and running an orphanage in the United Kingdom in the 1800s. He's also famous for never asking for any funding. The implication is, *Shouldn't you have the same faith as George?* What those same people pointing you to him either don't know or don't mention is that he held public events where he spoke with at least one orphan child on stage with him. He also was an anomaly. And, believe me, all of us who've raised support would love to have just sat in a room and prayed. We tried that, a lot. God wanted me to sit in front of people and ask them.

Because I needed to ask, God brought far more good things to us from the process than bad.

One of the greatest things that came from raising support are the amazing friends Ali and I would never have had without going through the process. It's one thing for someone to say he or she will pray for you, but when he or she is sending funds each month, I suspect the odds they will pray for you go way up. When one hundred families are on your support team, it feels more stable than a paycheck from a single entity.

I'll always be grateful for the advocacy from some of our supporters. For example, our insurance agent took me to lunch and *handwrote* referrals for me. Thanks, John. And our pastor in charge of spiritual gift testing said, "I can't give money, but I can refer you to people." I'm convinced he gave me names of people who scored high for the gift of giving. Thanks, Scott.

One hundred and thirty-three families gave Ali and me our launch. They are carved into our hearts forever with gratitude. We deeply love and appreciate them to this day.

That November in 2005 I hit that dreaded support-raising wall. It was in that moment I felt God saying it was time to resign and leave AT&T. Time to take another step of faith. God asking again, "Do you trust me?"

I flew to San Antonio to tell my boss I was resigning. He was very supportive. The awkward layoff and support conversations would come later. He offered for me to stay longer, but I was already mentally gone, and it was time to make it official. My last day would be at the end of November.

It worked out that my last day would be a Friday. I drove to our Richardson, Texas, office and handed my laptop and security badge to a nice young lady. I walked out of the turnstile doors, and it hit me, "I can't go back in." I had burned my ships. My regular paycheck was gone. We had two kids. At that time, Ali stayed home and worked a little out of the house. I hadn't finished raising support, and I couldn't officially start at e3 or draw a check from that support until I hit my one hundred percent mark.

I thought we'd have the biggest celebration that night. What a milestone. We were officially in midair of this leap of faith.

Instead, we got into a fight that lasted weeks.

Thus began a pattern we would fall into for years.

Ali and I married young. We had both just turned twenty-two, and we married at spring break during our senior year at college. What we know now is that we weren't formed emotionally. We each had brokenness we weren't unaware of. We packed that messiness into large bags and then attempted to hand those bags to one another to carry. Neither could carry the other's, despite how hard we tried. Ali tried much harder than me.

I was insecure, but as an allegedly strong guy who was a leader, I thought I was hiding my unhealth, when in fact I was leaking it all over everyone. Later I would realize that I had strength and weakness upside down.

Ali had her brokenness, and like a good married couple we hit each other perfectly in one another's weak spots. I would play out my insecurity with her. She would attempt to assuage me, that would fail, there would be anger, make up, repeat.

This leap of faith moment, however, became part of a pattern: Anytime we took a major faith step, or pressed into a dark place spiritually, Ali and I would get sideways. How much of that was our brokenness and flesh and how much was a spiritual enemy provoking us?

One day I'll find out.

This unresolved mess, insecurity, and occasional marital discord was running in the background when I got on an airplane and flew to Kigali, Rwanda. This is the meeting where I met David Kaya, and it would change the course of our lives.

PASTOR
DAVID KAYA

*Pastor David Kaya encouraging pastors in a
refugee camp in Maban, South Sudan.*

DAVID KAYA IS more than a friend; he's a brother. Our children are named for one another. My youngest daughter carries the name Kaya, and his son is my namesake. As of this writing, we're nearing twenty years together. His heart for God is indefatigable. He is God's gift to me. Without David's partnership, Empower One wouldn't exist, and I would have no story to tell you.

His name may appear more often in this book than any other, and with good reason. It's his perseverance, his knowledge, and his keen listening to the Holy Spirit that yielded Empower One.

In many ways, his story is the origin of our ministry.

While South Sudanese, David Kaya was born in the village of Erepi, Uganda, just outside of Moyo in the north, near the border of South Sudan. Because of war in Sudan, his family was sheltering in Uganda. He is one of eleven brothers and sisters. His father hails from the Madi tribe and his mother from the Kuku. His father was an Episcopal priest. David grew up in the church but didn't know Jesus.

Unfortunately, they weren't in Uganda long before the dictator Idi Amin rose to power. Amin is from northern Uganda, and his reign of terror began to affect David's family, so they crossed north and came back home to Sudan. In 1983, Sudan's government established Islamic law. This triggered the rebellion from the southerners and the civil war. Again, this war threatened David's family. *Again*, they crossed borders, this time back into northern Uganda, and set up life inside a refugee camp.

That last crossing was David's most harrowing. He recalls living near a large camp for internally displaced peoples in Sudan in 1986. His father took up residence near the camp to minister to the people inside. Later, speaking about that time in his life, David said, "It was a bright day like this very day. We didn't know that we were [be]seiged by the rebels of the Sudan People's Liberation Army (SPLA). They blocked our whole village and cut us off from rescue. . . . Before we could finish our lunch we heard a loud noise. . . . There was a heavy gun shot and explosions everywhere and they were targeting the refugees near us. . . . Many, many people were killed during that time."[2]

David was a teenager, so he was big enough to help carry his family's belongings. His mother took clothes and some of their most precious belongings and rolled them into a single-sized mattress. She assigned David to carry the mattress on his head. She gathered the family and said, "Let us just go. If it means for us to die, let us die. And if we could not die, let the children escape."

David continued, "So we escaped through the firing of bullets . . . and this was a journey of ninety-eight kilometers through the Nile Valley. That was the day I said, 'Lord save me! I need you now!'"

He recalls hiding and sleeping during the day and walking at night. They walked in a group, and he remembers how the group would move away from anyone with a cough or a crying baby. He recalled it raining and the mattress soaking up the water and becoming almost unbearably heavy. They had to fear both the Arab army of Sudan and the rebel soldiers of the SPLA.

In that same interview, David said, "God used that [experience] to turn my heart to look to him and not to the things of this earth. . . . I have a purpose of why I'm here. That became a starting point, and a turning point in my life and I started valuing God in all circumstances of my life. [This became] the beginning of our mission where I started thinking I need to preach the gospel and start leading many to Christ and start telling the good news of Jesus Christ. So that has been my mission and will be my mission until I depart here on earth."

Safe in a refugee camp in northern Uganda with his family, David finished secondary school. He was a good student, as were his brothers and sisters. He wanted to continue his education, but his family lacked the funds to send him to university.

---

2 "David Kaya's Story: A Profile," posted July 29, 2024, by Empower One, YouTube, https://www.youtube.com/watch?v=9QUi34cXwXg.

This is when he and a few friends ran into an American missionary from Kentucky named Harold Cathey. Harold sensed these guys were sharp and eager, so he asked if they would like to attend the seminary at which he taught in Jinja, Uganda. They jumped at the chance. David spent the next few years balancing a new marriage, odd jobs (the best being a pharmacy technician), and his studies at Global Theological Seminary (GTS) in Jinja. He moved from the Episcopal Church of Sudan to the upstart Baptists under Harold's mentorship.

Harold and his wife, Beverly, began to directly mentor and disciple David. Beverly explained the gospel in a way where it finally fully clicked for David. Harold baptized him. Harold drilled into David the importance of a healthy church, the role of a pastor as a shepherd, and the need to keep allegiance with God's word.

During a season of David working odd jobs to keep his young family afloat, Harold sent him back to northern Uganda with a mandate to strengthen the existing Baptist churches in that region and to start planting new ones.

At GTS, David had befriended a dynamic, entrepreneurial pastor and church planter. He got David work leading and teaching Key Man conferences organized by an American from Plano, Texas.

Finally, Nathan Sheets with e3 Partners entered David's life. Nathan had cocreated the EvangeCube. The same one I used in Beirut. Nathan was helping e3 open East Africa, and he was looking for faithful guys who could train others to use the EvangeCube. A friend of Nathan's referred David to him, and David soon became e3 Partners' EvangeCube Trainer for Sudan.

I said earlier that Empower One doesn't exist without David Kaya. Empower One doesn't exist without Nathan Sheets either. He would become the most essential American to making Empower One possible, which I'll share in a later chapter.

Because of Harold and Beverley, and because of Nathan—but mostly because of God—I met David Kaya.

I Don't Have Anything Like That

When I met David in 2005 at a conference in Kigali, Rwanda, I was working for e3 with Nathan. David was the last speaker at the conference, which had featured leaders from multiple East African countries, all extolling how well their church-planting work was going. Baby-faced and thin, David was in his early thirties, though he looked much younger. He represented Sudan. e3 had recently promoted him to country director.

He spoke bluntly, and his speech was different from those who had preceded him. "I don't have anything like these other testimonies. Four months ago, a twenty-three-year civil war ended in my country. I recently preached in a city in Sudan, and two people died while I was preaching. They carried two people on mats, and they died of malaria at the conference where I preached. We have no paved roads, no running water, no electricity. I have managed to plant eight new churches. I feel totally stuck. I have been publicly humiliated in my hometown. Other church leaders who do not preach the real gospel even slapped my face in town."

The atmosphere in the room changed. I was locked in on David and his testimony. Everyone in the room was moved by the challenges he faced. I spent the rest of the conference getting to know him.

We clicked.

A GIFT OF
THREE YEARS

STILL RUNNING ON fumes from jet lag from the Rwanda trip where I met David, I walked into my boss and mentor Mike Jorgensen's office at e3. He wanted me to work in Bolivia, but I also knew he had always been supportive of me and someone who listened to the Spirit of God. I asked him, "Mike, would you mind if I worked with David Kaya in Sudan?"

He said, "It's okay with me, but Sudan and David fall under Nathan Sheets. You'll need to ask Nathan."

I immediately walked down the hall and turned into Nathan's office. He had the coolest office at e3. A funky wooden desk, taxidermy on the walls, spears, swords, and all sorts of mementos from his travels. Nathan radiated energy. He's one of the most dynamic people I've ever met. He raised the most money for the ministry, but he also launched innovative initiatives. In addition to coinventing the EvangeCube, he was also a primary force behind the I Am Second campaign. On the side, he and his wife had a hobby: beekeeping. Eventually, it turned into a small local honey business. Today, that business has grown into Nature Nate's Honey.

He was personally generous. He was, and is, one of a kind. He taught me so much about fundraising. He had internalized his role as a catalyst to help kingdom-minded believers invest in God's kingdom. He led with his own giving, and he loved people well.

He became another mentor and a friend, and without him this story doesn't happen. He's also another believer who walks with a spiritual limp.

I waited until he downed his Spark drink, a caffeinated powder that helped his ADD brain focus. Then I asked him, "Hey man, I loved meeting David Kaya and loved his story. Honestly, I'm pretty drawn to the challenge he's facing. I know you're working with him, but I'd love to help and work with him if that's okay with you?"

"Yes!" Nathan almost shouted at me and pounded his desk. "Man, that would be awesome!" Then he leaned on his elbows on his desk toward me. "Mike, look, I wish I had the time to devote to David and his work what he needs, but I just don't. I think it would be awesome if you worked with him."

It was like a party exploded inside of me. I was ecstatic.

Nathan continued, "You need to meet Michael Radler. We were just in Rwanda, and God told him to work in Sudan. He's in Fort Worth, and you need to meet him. I'll set up a meeting and we'll go over there together."

A few weeks later, Nathan and I drove west to Fort Worth.

Michael is successful in the marketplace, and he has a beautiful family. But what stuck out to me is how tuned in he was with the Lord. He was another limp-walker, which made the connection easier, and he gave off the vibe of a guy who spent good amounts of time with God.

After getting to know one another, I learned he'd already met David Kaya. Then he turned to me in one of those first few meetings and said, "Mike, here's what I'll do. I'll help you and David get started. I'll help you guys for three years. I'll help you with some resources to start, but I'll only match what you raise for three years. After three years, that's it."

I said, "Thank you Michael, that means more than you know, and I'll take that deal."

God used Michael to give us the runway to start. After the plane was airborne for a while, we realized we needed to make a change, which would require another leap of faith. But first, it was time to go to David's homeland: South Sudan.

ALIEN SOIL

Rumbek, South Sudan, August 2006

The most interesting man in Africa's pet chimpanzee enjoying a Coca-Cola.

T COULD HAVE been the cantina bar from *Star Wars*.

Military contractors, UN soldiers, land mine removers, construction workers, foreign journalists, NGO workers, spies, and missionaries like us congregated in the rustic camp. I was on my first trip to Sudan, and I oscillated between being overwhelmed and intoxicated by the culture shock.

We encountered one of the most interesting men I'll ever meet, a young Kenyan who'd built the camp. He was the kind of guy who knew how to get things done even at this middle-of-nowhere outpost. If the right military contractor asked for a steak, he'd have a rib eye within two days. Or, his pièce de résistance was the swimming pool he installed. He had first sourced a pool shell, fixed it on a flatbed truck, and had it driven from Kenya to Rumbek. Upon arrival, the shell had cracked on the pothole-filled dirt roads. Undeterred, he dug a large hole and filled it with a rubber liner, and, voilà, the "hotel" within the camp had a swimming pool. We learned he owned a snake venom business. He and his brother started it in Kenya. They farmed the snakes and collected the venom for antidotes. We also learned when his personal funds got low, he'd fly to Dubai to earn extra cash as an underwater welder. A mentor had told him in his late teens he needed a skill. He chose underwater welding. We shared glass-bottled Coca-Colas with his three pet chimpanzees. And I'll never forget his goat, who found him every day at 5 p.m. and would gently head butt his leg until he fed the goat a daily cigarette.

Apparently everyone, even the goat, was on edge in that place. A twenty-three-year civil war had ended only the year before, and every local male over the age of fifteen openly carried a rifle. That was pretty wild, even for this Texan.

I didn't even have Chewbacca to cover me.

My First Power Encounter

Three days later, five of us stood on the side of Rumbek's main road. It was August, the middle of the rainy season. We learned we'd be trading the cooler weather the rains brought for mud and water-filled potholes that could swallow a small car. This main road was made of murram, a mixture of fine sand, gravel, and the area's red clay. I thought about Oklahoma's red soil. *Maybe this place isn't so different from what I know.* But, as more cows and goats passed us than vehicles, the thought evaporated.

Pastor Benjamin, a young church leader from Rumbek, had brought us here to show us the church he started. All I saw were the remnants of a market. A few naked bamboo poles still stood upright, the kind that shopkeepers used to set their awnings upon to create a pop-up marketplace. A massive mahogany tree sat behind the poles. Pastor Benjamin began, "This is where our church met, under this tree here. It was so good. This is a busy road so the people could find us easily. And this tree gave us a lot of good shade."

That roadside shade is a boon to marketplaces. When you're barely north of the equator and the afternoon sun bakes, shade is critical.

I was confused. "Pastor, does your church still meet here? It looks like a market."

"No." Benjamin told us the rest of the story. "The shopkeepers in this area saw our church meeting here. They became jealous of our place. They found the landowner and complained that such a good place was being used for our church."

Benjamin spoke with no anger or frustration. Just matter-of-factly recounting the events to us.

"The landowner found me and told me we had to find a new place to meet." Benjamin continued. "I told that man, 'We have an agreement. You should respect the church more than this.'"

The owner saw no sign from God, only dollar signs. Benjamin moved his small congregation to a new location.

The shopkeepers moved in, built their stalls, and filled them with soap, sesame seed snacks, sugar, petrol in water bottles, and other small items for the local community.

One week later, every leaf had fallen off the tree.

Without shade, the market failed. Pastor Benjamin was too kind to tell the landowner, "I told you so."

That was one of the first power encounters I experienced in South Sudan, a stark reminder of God's ultimate control. And, as you're about to read, it wouldn't be the last.

Far from it.

Polygamy as a Church-Planting Strategy

Pastor David and I returned to Rumbek with a team from a church in Plano, Texas, six months after that maiden trip. During our previous visit, we'd held a church-planting training over three days to see who among the local church leaders would catch the vision for church planting. A few men did, but our translator for that training grasped it better than all the others. This trip, our group was larger. I split our group between an area where we were starting a church and one where we were providing a few new churches with a push.

On our second night, we met with local church leaders inside their church. It had a five-foot-high mud wall for its exterior. On top was a grass roof held together by hand-cut wooden poles. We sat on wooden benches inside the church that was kept cool by the thick thatched roof. Isaac, our same translator who had caught the vision from our first training, sat with us.

Once our meeting officially began, Pastor Garang, the senior pastor from the established church we sat in, wasted no time in getting to the point. "We have a big problem. This man has planted two churches." He pointed at Isaac.

I looked over at David. He looked at me with no emotion. His face looked blank. We were early in our working relationship, but we had enough of a connection that I knew to stay quiet and wait for the other shoe to drop. I relied entirely on David in these situations. I was so new to not only Africa, but ministry in general that I needed his help. I looked at Pastor Garang, squinted my eyes, pursed my lips a little, and cocked my head to the side. *Starting two churches is a problem?*

Pastor Garang continued. "Isaac here has planted one church near the home of his first wife and the second church near the home of his second wife."

I didn't reply. I had no idea what to do or say. I was so new to ministry. I had no idea how to deal with polygamy. I started praying in my mind, asking God to help. I tried to keep a poker face and wait for God to bail me out of this situation. I hoped David had an answer for all of this.

Then the twice-married translator looked at David and spoke up. "This is why I am glad you are here. I did not know even what the Bible says about these things. I did not know you are only to take one wife. I took this second wife because my brother died, and my clan forced me to take this woman as my second wife."

Further context may be necessary: In virtually all the tribes in South Sudan, the long-held tradition of the wedding dowry drives this behavior. In his tribe, Dinka, a man pays a dowry to the family of the woman he wants to marry. The size and type of a dowry depends on tribe, geography, education, and a host of other factors. However, dowries often exceed a young man's resources. In my time of operating in South Sudan, dowries have grown to the outrageous. For example, a young man with no assets who may earn between $50 and $350 (US) per month is routinely requested to offer a dowry of $20,000 or more. Extended family members also add to the list. For example, an uncle and aunt may want twelve cows and $2,000. Another aunt may ask for new plates, a cousin for bedsheets, another uncle for five additional cows, and on and on it goes.

The process generally goes like this: A young man takes an interest in a young lady. He sets a meeting with her parents, and this meeting typically involves quite a few more family members. The man states his desire to marry the woman. Sometimes the young lady's family has prepared for this meeting and presents him with their dowry demands. Other times, they'll present their demands in a subsequent meeting.

The young man takes this dowry demand back to his extended family. They agree to pool their resources to help him. His parents, uncles, aunts, siblings, and so forth contribute. He returns to the young lady's family with the dowry or he negotiates with her family. They may reduce the dowry or agree to let them proceed to marriage, but with the expectation that he will pay the dowry in full over time.

Several issues arise because of this dowry system.

First, violence. Among the cattle-keeping tribes of South Sudan, cows are the most prized asset. Dowries within these tribes are primarily cows. If the young man and his family do not have enough cows, his friends—typically all young men—will band together to raid and steal another tribe's cows to pay the dowry. Both the attacking thieves and the defending cattle keepers often kill one another in these raids. These raids lead to revenge attacks and killings, a cycle of violence that continues today. Typically the violence ends when either the chiefs step in and negotiate peace or the government sends the army to quell the fighting.

Second, women are treated as property. In my example above, we in the West may relate somewhat because it appears to involve romance between a young man and woman. This certainly occurs in South Sudan; however, in some cases a father will sell his daughter to a man who can pay a large dowry. The Lost Boys who came to America in the late '90s and early 2000s drove some dowries to ludicrous heights after making money in America. These are the South Sudanese refugees who received lottery visas to immigrate to the United States during that time period. They primarily came from a large refugee camp in Kenya called Kakuma. They got jobs in the United States that provided them the funds to pay larger dowries back home. In other cases, the unions are less about romance and more about families or clans connecting through marriage alliances.

In normal circumstances, the young man's family rallies and pools their resources to help him pay the dowry. After the wedding, the woman moves to her new husband's home. In some cases, the extended family communicates to the new bride that *she* owes *them* because of their dowry contribution. She's made to cook, clean, gather firewood, and take care of children for the extended family, in addition to her husband, to pay off what they see as her debt. She's also expected to produce children to pay off her debt. The family will want males, but they want females to make their money back. Why is that? When *her* daughter is approached for marriage, her husband's family will bring *their* list of demands to those young suitors. If her husband's father contributed ten cows to bring her into the family, he will use his granddaughter's marriage proposal to make back his ten and will probably ask for fifteen to profit more. And on and on it goes.

This dowry system is why Isaac's clan forced him to marry his deceased brother's wife and to produce children with her. They had invested a significant amount of resources to acquire her for his brother. They could only make their cows and money back if she produced daughters they could marry off in order to recoup their investment. Isaac was under pressure to ensure his family could be made whole again through his brother's wife as well as through his first wife.

When all of this came out during our meeting, I was surprised by Isaac's reaction. He was contrite. He said, "Brothers, I am feeling ashamed. This lady of my late brother, I really did not want to marry her. I worked very hard for the dowry for my first wife, and I care for her. My real wife is very upset with the family, and this wife of my brother, she is not really accepting this marriage yet. I cannot send her away. This is the way we do things here. And now Pastor David, you have explained to me the Bible." Then Isaac added with emotion, tapping his index finger on the arm of his chair, "And did you know my clan even asked me to marry a third lady? But I refused. How can I even care for these two now?"

Ultimately, we physically moved the churches and assigned new leaders for each of them. Isaac voluntarily went under church discipline, with Pastor Garang overseeing a program of biblical education. As a believer, Isaac's situation was complicated. Garang would teach Isaac that he could not simply leave the second wife. Casting her out as a widow on top of an abandoned or divorced wife would expose her to a life of danger, misery, and potential destitution. That would not honor God. He would have to live with the consequences and make the best of them. He would not be able to hold a leadership position in the church, and Garang would have Isaac warn and implore the young, unmarried men in the church to only marry one wife.

The thorny problem of our polygamy-based church-planting strategy was solved, and Isaac became a catalyst for a major shift in our ministry. After this incident with Isaac, David pulled me aside.

"Mike, we have to change this approach. We cannot find trained leaders who are ready to lead churches. We must build them ourselves."

We stopped everything we were doing and prayed. We asked God what he wanted us to do. The methodology we were trained on and trying to use didn't work in the Sudan context. That period of prayer led us to start North East Africa Theological Seminary (NEATS) the following month.

David joined with Edward Dima and gathered seventeen men under three trees in Kajo Keji, South Sudan. That was our first class of NEATS church planters. From that moment on, we would try to keep our hands and hearts open to wherever God led us to reach unreached people in Sudan and South Sudan.

But before we talk about that, what do you know about Sudan?

ALAS, OH LAND OF WHIRRING WINGS WHICH LIES BEYOND THE RIVERS OF CUSH

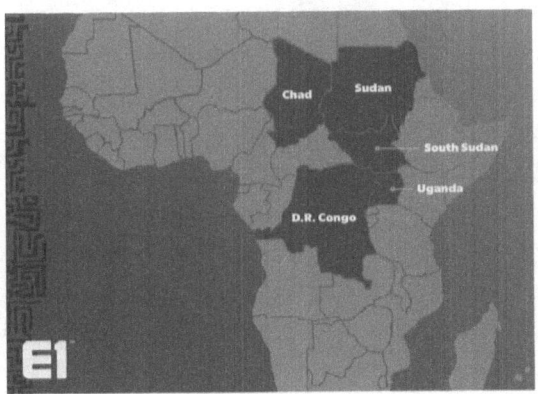

Boundaries of Empower One's African operations.

THE FIRST TIME I went to Africa, I'm not sure I knew Sudan existed or where it was located. US schools rarely teach the history of Sudan, so here's a short primer on the background of this war-torn country. The first lesson is now it is two countries, Sudan and South Sudan.

The original, undivided Sudan sits directly south of Egypt, with Ethiopia to its east and Chad to its west. Southeast, you'll find Kenya, and its southern border touches Uganda, DR Congo, and Central Africa Republic to its southwest. Those southern borders now touch South Sudan. The White Nile runs through both South Sudan and Sudan, and the Blue Nile enters from Ethiopia. Both rivers meet in Khartoum before heading north to Egypt.

Until 2011, Sudan was the largest country in Africa. In that year, South Sudan gained independence, separating from Sudan and becoming the 194th country in the world. South Sudan is about the size of Texas. The North and South had been at odds for hundreds of years. The North's implementing of Sharia, or Islamic law, in 1983 was the final transgression that sparked the South's revolt.

Since Empower One's inception, David and I have navigated South Sudan's first civil war, which kicked off in December 2013 and only cooled in 2021. And in April 2023, Sudan erupted in its own devastating civil war, which we're still traversing as of this writing.

Why work in such an unstable, violent place?

Because this is the exact place and these are the exact people who need the transformative life change and peace only Jesus can provide. The places in the world, like Sudan, where unreached peoples live are unreached for a reason. It's difficult, dangerous, expensive, spiritually dark, full of strongholds, and often physically hard to reach. We're choosing to do the hard things. We have a God who can do anything. Isn't it more fun and stimulating to be in this faith-space with God, regardless of the challenges?

Secondly, the worse the situation, the greater the gospel opportunity. Again, I abhor these wars and the needless sufferings caused by selfish, evil men. However, we have been able to meet refugees at their darkest hours, and we've extended comfort and love to them. When we help with a little food, tools for their garden, or someone to talk with, we get to be God's hands and feet. We get to show God's love for them, and ultimately, show them God's kingdom, which is not of this evil, broken world.

I loathe the senseless wars my friends in these countries have endured in modern times. I've sat with these same friends when they had thousand-yard stares from the severe, traumatic events they encountered firsthand from fighting. The scale of violence perpetrated toward women is beyond heartbreaking.

There is a spiritual level of evil that feels breathtaking. I'm convinced Satan's Number Two or Three is seated above this region. In modern Cush, it feels like we are at war not only "against the rulers, against the authorities, against the cosmic powers over this present darkness, against the spiritual forces of evil in the heavenly places" (Eph. 6:12), but, indeed, against *actual* flesh and blood. Or, at least we are continually caught up in it.

Sudan Is in the Bible

"Alas, oh land of whirring wings
Which lies beyond the rivers of Cush,
Which sends envoys by the sea,
Even in papyrus vessels on the surface of the waters.
Go, swift messengers, to a nation tall and smooth,
To a people feared far and wide,
A powerful and oppressive nation

Whose land the rivers divide."
—Isaiah 18:1–2

Sudan's history is as old as Egypt's. In the Old Testament, Cush is modern-day Sudan. You can visit pyramids near the Egyptian border built as far back as 800 BC. At some point in the sixth century AD, Christianity entered and flourished. One might say from the seventh century AD to this very day, Christianity and Islam have clashed inside modern-day Sudan and South Sudan.

In the 1890s, the British entered the scene, and in 1899 Sudan became a British colony. Charles Gordon would achieve infamy in Great Britain for his fight with the *Mahdi* of Sudan. Winston Churchill fought near Khartoum in 1898 and wrote a book about it called *The River War.*

In 1956, Sudan gained its independence from Great Britain. They began with a democratic government but quickly devolved into coups, a dalliance with communism, a war over an attempt to dig a canal in today's South Sudan, radical Islam, and, in 1983, a civil war with the southerners that would last until 2005.

Two southerners, armed only with bows and arrows, triggered this civil war when they shot Sudanese Army soldiers in Torit, South Sudan. Not only did this start a civil war between the north and south, it became a regional proxy war between communists and capitalist democracies, Arabs and Black Africans, and Arab countries and Israel.

In 1989, Omar al-Bashir led a bloodless coup in Khartoum and seized control of Sudan. He funded rigid Islamists, controlled the northern part of the country with an iron fist, and warred against the southerners. He also funded a rebel group called the Janjaweed, who terrorized the Darfurians on the western side of Sudan. That terror group, the Janjaweed, rebranded as the Rapid Support Forces and is fighting the Sudan army in the Sudan civil war as of this writing. In 2008, Bashir expelled every western missionary from Sudan.

The leader of the SPLA was a dynamic man by the name of John Garang. (No direct relation to Pastor Garang.) Garang received an economics degree from Grinnell College in Iowa. He turned down an offer for graduate school at University of California, Berkeley, opting instead to study agricultural economics in Tanzania.

In 1983, when the war began in Sudan, Garang led the fight. He would flip from communism to Western democracy during the course of the war, aligning with the stronger outside sponsor. With the support of Israel, the United States, Norway, and Great Britain, Garang led a ragtag group of rebels from near-total defeat to Bashir's capitulation in 2005. That year, Sudan and the SPLA signed the Comprehensive Peace Agreement (CPA), which stipulated that the south would immediately have a semiautonomous government until 2011. In 2011, the south voted for independence, which passed with ninety-nine percent of the people voting in favor.

The cost of this civil war was staggering. Two million people were killed and four million were displaced from their homes. When I brought short-term mission teams in 2006 through 2010, I asked the participants to note how many men they encountered over the age of forty. I did this because there were so few. Almost a generation of men were wiped out. This tragic fact directly impacted the approach that David and I took to church planting.

Unfortunately, only months after signing the CPA, Garang died in a helicopter crash. South Sudan might be quite different had he lived to lead its founding. Instead, two of his SPLA military deputies squared off in an election for president in 2011: Salva Kiir and Riek Machar. Kiir is from the dominant Dinka tribe. Machar is from the large Nuer tribe. Kiir won the contest and took the presidency. Machar became the first vice president.

Then December 15, 2013, arrived.

What really happened that day remains cloudy. On the record, President Kiir claimed that Machar attempted to assassinate him in

South Sudan's capital city of Juba. Machar fled the city and mobilized his Nuer tribe, particularly a militia called the White Army, to fight Kiir and the SPLA. There are sixty-four tribes in South Sudan. Most chose a side, and fighting broke out throughout the country. This conflict displaced 2.1 million people, and 1.5 million South Sudanese fled into refugee camps in northern Uganda alone. Consequently, Empower One became a refugee ministry from 2014 until 2021. But what Satan meant to steal, kill, and destroy, God used to bring hundreds of thousands to knowledge of him and tens of thousands to place their faith in him.

But we'll get to that later. Now, back to the early years of the ministry.

SEEING GOD'S KINGDOM AND PEOPLE IN CHAINS

IN THE SPRING of 2007, I was sitting with a man a bit older than me who was leading a foundation helping with various projects in South Sudan. I told him what I was experiencing. "I feel crazy and this might sound crazy. But I feel like there's this whole spiritual world I can see now."

He nodded, so I kept going.

"I'm also seeing this image at churches in the United States. I feel like I'm seeing people dragging heavy chains behind them. It's like Jesus took their chains and weights of sin. So I'm not talking about that, and I'm not trying to sound judgmental. But it's like I see them take on new chains that are the weights of extrabiblical expectations and pressures instead of living totally free in Christ."

He looked me in the eyes and just said, "You're not crazy."

I exhaled in relief. I'd found a kindred spirit who understood what I was feeling.

Today, experiencing more of God's kingdom while on earth feels like a gift. C. S. Lewis wrote, "Enemy-occupied territory—that is what this world is. Christianity is the story of how the rightful king has landed, you might say landed in disguise and is calling us to take part in a great campaign of sabotage."[3] My work felt more and more like this campaign of kingdom sabotage.

Midway through my second year working in South Sudan, I felt as if I'd stepped into another dimension, as if God were giving me glimpses into his invisible kingdom here on earth. I began to experience "the authorities, cosmic powers, and spiritual forces of evil" Paul had written about in Ephesians 6. (I hadn't run into those working at AT&T, at least that I know of. I had a few bosses I still wonder about.)

In the West, we try to separate and contain the spiritual from the rest of our lives, whether that's our vocation, our emotions, or how we relate to others. Hence, a common comment you hear is, "My faith is private." In South Sudan, the spiritual is fully integrated into everything. No one tries to split it out. When your child is sick, you consult a witch doctor.

I had entered a power culture: Whose spirit or god has the most power? Time and again, I experienced God using power displays to make himself known. I saw demon possession firsthand and continually experienced the power of prayer. We would pray and God would miraculously work things out or bring people "out of nowhere" to help us or solve the problems we faced.

---

3 C. S. Lewis, *Mere Christianity* (New York: HarperOne, 2012), 45–46.

Does God Care About the Person in the Middle of Nowhere?

What about the person in the middle of nowhere? Does God care about him or her? What if no one is around to tell them about Jesus? It's one of the classic questions about God.

The answer I experienced was this: He sends a flooring company owner.

The big, bright North Star for Empower One is to bring the good news of Jesus to those who've never heard his name. God has called us to a particular part of the world: South Sudan, Sudan, DR Congo, Chad, and one country we can't name publicly.

In August of 2006, I was sitting in a restaurant in Nairobi with Bob Funk, my friend and traveling partner. He'd come with me on my first ever South Sudan trip. We were there to meet a missionary couple who lived in South Sudan. They lived in Rumbek at that time. They were mixing meetings with a little R&R in Kenya's capital city. Over roasted meat, sitting outside with low lighting, the missionary told us about the Toposa tribe in far southeastern South Sudan. He said, "I really want to engage and reach them, but I don't have the bandwidth or resources. You guys should go and check out that area."

With the funding secured from the gentleman in Fort Worth, we chartered a small plane with Mission Aviation Fellowship (MAF) in December of 2006. We flew around South Sudan looking for good contacts and inroads to unreached tribes.

I landed in Nairobi and met David. My bag didn't make it, and we didn't have time to wait for its arrival. We befriended a taxi driver. When he learned I didn't have my luggage, he lent me two shirts and drove me to a store to pick up a few toiletries. I flew into South Sudan with two extra shirts and what I was wearing.

We first went to a village called Lietnom. Locals met us on the dirt airstrip with only a tractor for transportation. During that tractor ride, I witnessed firsthand the desperation of the people. The sun set as we rode toward where we were staying. I grabbed a flashlight and pointed it down the road to help the driver. My light found a few women on their hands and knees on the road, scooping water from a puddle of a tire divot into a jerry can. It had recently rained, and they were gathering what water they could, because so few clean water wells were available.

My further welcome to South Sudan.

Our last stop was Kapoeta, where the missionary had suggested we go to learn about the Toposa tribe. We didn't know anyone there. I had found a water drilling company with lodging and had booked tukuls for David and me. Their driver picked us up in a small Toyota Hilux. We dropped our things in our concrete tukuls and talked about what to do next.

We walked about half a mile into town and found a church. I wasn't sure how to square finding a church in a town surrounded by Toposa who were believed to be unreached. I'd later learn that the congregations in town were made up of foreign NGO workers. We found three pastors sitting outside, talking. They pulled out plastic chairs, offered tea, and we began to have small talk.

Within just a few moments, David and one of the pastors realized they knew one another from their time in a refugee camp in Uganda. In an instant, we had credibility and connection. Smiles and hand-shakes broke out, and we got down to business.

I asked the pastors, "How many Toposa attend any of these churches in town?"

"Zero," they replied.

I followed up with another question. "Okay, well then how many mature Christian believers would you say you're even aware of among the Toposa?"

There was a long pause. "There is one guy."

One.

A 2010 census estimated there to be around 350,000 Toposa.

Eventually, we met the "one." British missionaries had raised him in Uganda. With the recent civil war ending, he had come back to his people. He had opened a school and was focused on helping kids.

From there, we started working with the Toposa. We found believers among the neighboring Turkana tribe just across the border in Kenya. Toposa and Turkana speak a similar dialect and can understand one another. A big issue with reaching unreached people is not having believers to translate. But the Turkana solved that problem, initially. We'd go on to send our own indigenous missionaries to live with the Toposa, and we'd bring a few to attend NEATS. We also started bringing Americans over on short-term mission trips.

One of those trip-goers was Robert Gunn. He and his wife Jane owned and operated a flooring company that specialized in tile and stone throughout central and south Texas.

Robert was an older gentleman when he came on my trip. One day he was walking in a village and met another older gentleman named Orochu. Through a translator, they struck up a conversation. Robert shared the good news of Jesus with Orochu. He asked Orochu, "Do you want to put your trust in, and follow, Jesus?"

Orochu said, "I used to worship many spirits and my ancestors. And then I observed this river and that mountain and I thought, 'There has to be one god.' Since that day I have only worshiped one God and today He has sent you to me to tell me the rest of his story."

Orochu's reply recalls Romans 1:19–20: "For what can be known about God is plain to them, because God has shown it to them. For his invisible attributes, namely, his eternal power and divine nature, have been clearly perceived, ever since the creation of the world, in the things that have been made."

Orochu then took Robert to his home, where Orochu gathered his family and had them sit down. Surrounded by around thirty people, Orochu told Robert to tell them about Jesus. Another older man was a part of that group. He took Robert to his home, gathered his family, and said the same thing: "Robert, you tell them about God and Jesus."

This wonderful series of events reminds me of Acts 17:26–27: "And He made from one man every nation of mankind to live on all the face of the earth, having determined their appointed times and the boundaries of their habitation, that they would seek God, if perhaps they might grope for Him and find Him, though He is not far from each one of us."

So what happens to the person in the middle of nowhere?

God hears his cry and sends his messenger.

And sometimes that messenger sells tile and stone flooring.

LEADING WITH NO VISION

School children heading home after a long day at school.
The original flagship church is in the background.

N THE EARLY years with e3, God didn't give David or me a big vision for the ministry. We felt called to reach the unreached in South Sudan and Sudan, but we didn't sense God giving us anything more specific or grand. God would only give us the next step. For example, to start NEATS.

We weren't frustrated by this; however, it did make it challenging when discussing the ministry with pastors and leaders in America. They wanted us to pull out maps and to have a plan to reach all the unreached tribes. A foundational element in good leadership is to have a vision. A vision unifies your team, excites your supporters, and lifts your accomplishments. We would have to wait six years before God gave us the first vision, and it wouldn't be until 2021 that God would give us a vision for flagship churches.

During those first six years, we plodded along, only focusing on the next step. When we looked up after those initial years, David's original eight churches had grown to one hundred and forty.

We also fell in love with primary and secondary schools. In 2007, David took the budget for NEATS and stretched it to start a primary (or elementary) school in Kajo Keji. I was skeptical and thought this represented mission drift. However, one of our key principles is that we are locally led. David had successfully gotten NEATS off the ground and was able to manage the primary school, so I supported him.

Schools kept popping up as a strategic tool to not only reach, disciple, and educate the next generation but also as a way to show communities we loved them.

In our regional leader John Monychol's home village of Baliet, there was only a low-performing government school and an Islamic school in 2010. One of John's closest disciples taught English *at* the Islamic school. They wanted to start a small Christian primary school. John deeply wanted a Christian alternative to the Islamic school. Muslim funding from the Middle East built schools like this to evangelize and indoctrinate children. They also offered free schooling in Sudan, and some families would send their children to Sudan for a better education. These kids almost always ended up in madrassas, where they only memorized the Koran.

A family from Dallas, Texas, provided the funds, and we started the school John was clamoring for in a mud-walled building with a grass roof. They put a flagpole out front for assembling each morning. Within six months, that school transformed John's church and the community. The people loved that a Christian school had begun. Many people started coming to the church and a lot found Jesus. I visited Baliet both before and after the school was in place. When I visited after the school had started, the community's reaction to me totally changed. It went from a bit cold and distant to warm, happy, and excited.

Jackson Mogga was a South Sudanese missionary we sent to Kagwada, South Sudan. When he arrived, the people were cold to him too, and he had a tough time starting a church. No one was interested in coming to his church. Jackson switched strategies. He started cutting children's hair and telling them Bible stories. Second, he was a trained teacher, so we encouraged him to start a small school for kids grades one through four. Once again, everything changed. The local chiefs granted him fifty acres for a school, many people started coming to his church, and many got saved.

The light bulb came on for me. Every parent knows, if you love my kids, I love you. We had figured out how to pair a small, rural school with a church plant and make that work.

We were hooked on schools. They show a community you care for and love them, they give kids a better opportunity in life, and our schools are explicitly Christian. The kids who attend learn God's word, the good news of the gospel, and we disciple them to follow Jesus. David's vision is for these kids to become the next generation of government and business leaders in South Sudan.

God opened a door into Darfur as well. Darfur is a large state in western Sudan and is ninety-eight percent Muslim. We had been praying for years for the best way to enter that state; however, God never gave us an opening we felt peace with until 2010. A missionary living in Malakal sent a disciple of hers, Silas (not his real name), to NEATS. Silas began integrating and learning until we hosted a twelve-hundred-pastor-strong conference in Kajo Keji. At that conference, I preached and challenged everyone to operate like Abraham, whose faith was immediate, costly, and radical. I had simply copied a teaching exactly as I heard and learned it from a missionary named Curtis Sergeant, whose training I had attended earlier.

Silas heard this and was back in Darfur within two months. A short time later, fearing for his life, he brought thirty Darfurians to NEATS, where they would live and learn for two years. At the end of those two years, they went all over the world: Iraq, Indonesia, Germany, Turkey, America, Sudan, and South Sudan.

We were getting established. NEATS was growing. We were continuously bringing short-term missionaries over. We added a farm that the students were required to work at in lieu of tuition. We were starting churches and baptizing hundreds of new believers. We were also forming our missiology.

OUR MISSIOLOGY

FOR THE MISSIONS geeks, let's get a little technical. (If you just like the story, skip ahead to the next chapter.) None of what you're reading works without David Kaya. As to why David is so critical, let's talk missiology.

Within this story about how God uses ordinary people is a missiological model called a nonresidential missionary model. Basically, we, the Americans, don't live full time on the mission field.

To be clear, I absolutely believe there is still a place for residential missionaries. However, in my sliver of missions, which is primarily church planting, I think the trend is moving in the nonresidential direction. Even when you study the life of the apostle Paul, he discipled, trained, equipped, and appointed *local* leaders to lead the churches.

There's a trend in international church planting, particularly among practitioners who plant to reach unreached or unengaged tribes, called disciple-making movements (DMMs). This was preceded by a methodology called church-planting movements (CPMs). David and I had the fortune to meet most of the leaders of the CPM methodology and sit in on several of their trainings. I love these guys. You'll be hard-pressed to find more dedicated, sold-out individuals operating in the kingdom than these men and women. Many have sacrificed tremendously, and they deserve a ton of our honor and respect.

As Teddy Roosevelt might say, "They're in the arena."[4]

While I use Paul as a biblical example of, essentially, a nonresidential church-planting missionary who didn't stay in one place very long, many of the CPM (and now DMM) practitioners move with *too* much rapidity in many cases. They empower church leaders too quickly. It is the "Goldilocks and the Three Bears" principle: not too fast, but not too slow. David and I have tried to incorporate as many of their tools and practices as possible, but we move *much* slower. The pastor in David cares deeply about church health; the driver in me wants to move fast to reach more tribes. It's a beautiful, healthy tension.

The bottom line is, if we want to move the needle to reach un-reached tribes and people groups, we're going to need to *empower local, near-culture* believers. A residential missionary can't want to run their program only through their converts or local believers. DMMers can't go so fast that entire regions get inoculated to the gospel.

We need to find or create believers who are going to do the work anyway, with or without any outside help—like we have with NEATS. Then we give them rocket fuel through the resources we have access to. That mostly means money. It's hard, messy, and you give up control. As a nonresidential missionary, you often miss out on the fun part of missions: time in the villages watching the birth of new churches, seeing the baptisms of new believers, or pioneering new areas that lack churches or even believers. Local believers have these experiences while you're in the background, sometimes thousands of miles away. But what is paramount? Your experience, or what's most effective in bringing the gospel to those who've never heard?

Now, back to our story.

---

4 TRCP Staff, "It Is Not the Critic Who Counts," *TRCP Blog*, Theodore Roosevelt Conservation Partnership, January 18, 2011, https://www.trcp.org/2011/01/18/it-is-not-the-critic-who-counts/.

AGAINST THE COSMIC POWERS OVER THIS PRESENT DARKNESS

IN JANUARY 2008, the team I was leading in Yei, South Sudan, may have thought I was bringing them into a literal, physical sabotage campaign. Shortly after dark, gunshots began popping off across the city. Like in a firefight, gunfire seemed to invite more gunfire, and it multiplied from varying distances. When we heard the resounding boom of a .50-caliber gun, some of the team dove under their beds.

Were we under attack?

No, it was New Year's Eve, and the locals were partying with AK-47s instead of fireworks. The next morning, we had bleary eyes and a deep desire for coffee and tea.

Despite gunfire (and one couple running from a swarm of bees), five members of that short-term mission team quit their jobs after that trip and entered full-time vocational ministry.

The first were David and Missy Williams. They had just gone through the Perspectives course and were primed for mission. Perspectives is a fifteen-session training that seeks to awaken Christ followers "to pursue the fulfillment of God's global purpose within every people for His glory."[5] At the end of their trip, a group of young women they had gotten to know asked them for a sewing machine. One woman said, "I'm not looking for a handout. If I could just get a sewing machine, I can put my children in school." The conversation rocked the Williams' world.

They came home, and Missy threw herself into research mode. In 2009, they launched a microfinance ministry under our ministry umbrella. Missy left her interior design business in Dallas, and, as you read in Part 1, she and David launched Seed Effect. They quickly outgrew our umbrella.

In 2016, in response to the war and hyperinflation, they shifted from microfinance to savings groups. They also had to leave South Sudan, so they pivoted to serving refugees. They had their fill of skeptics who didn't believe you could create successful savings groups among refugees. They don't have any money, right? As of this writing, they've saved over $11 million and grown small businesses throughout refugee settlement camps. Today, there's no better savings group and economic empowerment ministry serving refugees in the world.

Chris Cotner was another. He paused practicing law and helped start Water4 with Dick Greenly from Oklahoma City. They not only brought clean water to places all over the world, but they also empowered local people to drill and set up drilling businesses themselves. Karlis Gruzins and Salti Little each joined domestic ministries in Texas and Arkansas, respectively.

Perhaps God moving so powerfully caused a reaction in the spiritual realms—which informs what happened next.

---

5 "God's Purpose," Perspectives USA, https://perspectives.org/gods-purpose/.

Demons in Dreams

After enjoying New Year's by gunshot, a smaller group of us, including my father, visited Kajo Keji. We ended the trip by flying down to Entebbe, Uganda, where we planned to catch our international flight home. I shared a room with Jim Menne. Jim's wife had been my wife's roommate in college. We're fortunate that Jim and I became friends. Not all wives' husbands click. Jim had done evangelism in Yei, then he rode along the DR Congo's border with South Sudan into Kajo Keji. There he taught at NEATS, which wasn't even a year old.

That night in Entebbe, I had what started out as a nightmare, but, in my experience, it felt very real.

I shifted from sleep to awake. The room was pitch black, I couldn't move, and I felt a large, evil, dark force on my chest pressing against me.

I tried to roll over and wake Jim up to ask him to pray for me, but I couldn't move. I could only move my eyes. Even my mouth was paralyzed, so I couldn't cry out or yell or ask Jim to help.

In my mind, I cried out to Jesus saying, "In the name of Jesus and through the power of His blood, leave!" I repeated that over and over.

As quickly as it started, it vanished.

I was so at peace that I didn't even wake Jim up.

At breakfast, I told Jim what had happened. He listened intently. When I finished, he said, "Well, whatever that was left you and came to me." He'd had had the exact same experience right after me.

I'm aware of the phenomenon of sleep paralysis and that this fits that description. If that's what happened, it's odd that Jim had the same phenomenon. I'd never experienced something like that before entering ministry. I've since had this happen four other times. Each occurrence happened after Empower One made some form of headway toward reaching the unreached.

A Wicked Priest

Charlatans are everywhere.

In 2 Corinthians 11, Paul first mocks a group he calls "super-apostles." Later in the chapter, he gives it to the Corinthians straight: "For such men are false apostles, deceitful workers, disguising themselves as apostles of Christ. No wonder, for even Satan disguises himself as an angel of light. Therefore it is not surprising if his servants also disguise themselves as servants of righteousness, whose end will be according to their deeds." (vv. 13–15).

When you work in an unreached area, you get to experience what the first-century church experienced—both the good and the bad. The same can be said even for underreached areas, places where the gospel either barely exists or there's little biblical literacy and fewer churches.

A lot of what we ran into in our early years, and we continue to run into today, is simply a lack of information or training. This was the case with the polygamous translator in the earlier chapter. Recall that when confronted with his polygamous marriage, he told David (in an almost confessing tone) that he didn't know what the Bible taught about polygamy. Where we work, many so-called church leaders fall into this category. It's a big reason we started NEATS.

In other cases, we find "deceitful workmen."

On another trip I led one summer, I divided the team into three groups and sent them to different villages. Each team visited homes near a brand-new church plant under a tree. They engaged the community, shared the gospel, and prayed for people at their homes.

In one village, they kept hearing the same story: The people prayed in a nearby church and a priest wrote their names in the book of life.

Our team dug a bit further, asking what, exactly, they meant. They replied, "We go to [redacted]'s church to pray. He has a book of life. We pay him eight pounds and he writes our names in this book. He told us we would go to heaven."

He carried with him a literal book with the title *The Book of Life*. And eight South Sudanese pounds, at that time, was about $2 USD. Upon payment, he penciled or inked their names into his book and assured them of paradise after death.

If this priest knew Jesus, he was choosing to ignore him. More likely, he took the reverence the South Sudanese people show priests and pastors and used it to prey on his neighbors. Offering something via a witch doctor to your ancestors or a local spirit was normal. The priest took this normal practice and leveraged it for fairly small financial gain.

Months of evangelism with the real gospel of Jesus Christ and the establishment of a Bible-teaching church nearby put the wicked priest out of business.

But, like charlatans, evil is everywhere—a hungry lion looking for someone to devour (1 Peter 5:8).

The Exorcist

Spoiler alert: the finale of this story.

It was exactly as if I'd stepped onto a movie set.

Suddenly, this small woman in a wheelchair started to growl. I was holding onto one of her arms. It immediately became stiff as a board. I felt her become incredibly strong. Her voice changed to that raspy, evil bass, and she drooled as if she had rabies.

We prayed and hung on.

I was in our headquarters town of Kajo Keji. I'd brought over Americans on a short-term trip. I had tagged along with a couple to go out into a village for evangelism. We arrived at a home, a tukul with walls of mud and a dried-grass roof. This tukul was round; a few are square. We were in a forested area, and I recall appreciating the abundant shade.

The family was happy to receive visitors. They brought out chairs. On the ground lay a tarp with okra and cassava drying in the sun. Chickens pecked for bugs and goats bleated and picked at leaves on nearby bushes. Only women and children were home. Shortly after sitting and introducing ourselves, one woman began to nurse her baby.

I was positioned behind an American couple because I wanted them to take the lead in the conversation. As we began to talk, Kenyi, a South Sudanese translator and local church member, walked behind me. He touched my shoulder, leaned down, and asked me to come with him.

When we got out of earshot, he pointed to a woman about thirty yards away in a similar home as the one we'd just left. She was in a wheelchair. Kenyi told me she was possessed by a demon and had been terrorizing her neighbors, continually picking fights with them, and disturbing them at night.

I had encountered demon-possessed people before, but what came next was brand new.

We walked to her home and sat down with her. Her name was Christine. Kenyi had been talking with her. He talked through her behavior with her neighbors. She would terrorize them, and they were a mixture of angry and scared of her. Kenyi had shared the gospel with her. When he said the name of Jesus, a demon manifested. Hence his reason for grabbing me. Kenyi needed a prayer partner and wanted to invoke Matthew 18:20: "For where two or three have gathered together in My name, I am there in their midst." He looked at me and said, "Let's lay hands on her and pray."

I had encountered a demon-possessed woman in Ethiopia the year prior, and upon saying Jesus's name, that demon manifested as well. In that instance, the demon had controlled the woman, and she made money giving the fortunes it provided. It also threatened to kill her if she talked with us. We ended up walking away. Even with that experience under my belt, I was both confident in Jesus and nervous.

I took a quick inventory in my mind: Did I have any secret sin I needed to confess? Anything a demon or Satan could credibly accuse me of? David Kaya had taught me that, typically, he and his disciples would pray and confess sins before confronting a demon. I had less than thirty seconds. I felt like I was okay and followed Kenyi's lead.

I took her right side, Kenyi her left. I put one hand on her shoulder and the other on her arm. At the first mention of Jesus Christ, she stiffened, growled, and drooled. Like I said, I felt like I was in a movie. You know *that voice*. Well, I heard *that voice* talk. We kept praying, crying out to Jesus, and asking for the demon to leave her through the power of Jesus's blood. We prayed for almost ten minutes.

All at once, she went limp.

Her voice returned. She looked exhausted. She asked for water.

I handed her my liter-and-a-half plastic bottle of water.

She tipped it to her lips and emptied all of it. She expressed deep relief.

After pausing and comforting her for a bit, we explained the gospel again and asked if she wanted now to be filled with the Spirit and to follow Jesus.

She did, and she moved from the kingdom of darkness to the kingdom of light.

Later that week, I stood on the bank of a stagnant pool of water and prayed Luke 10:19: "Behold, I have given you authority to tread on serpents and scorpions, and over all the power of the enemy, and nothing will injure you.."

After praying that verse, I took my shoes off and slid into a pool of muddy water, about the size of a large swimming pool. I stepped slowly on the thick, sticky clay floor until the water reached just above my waist.

Two men carefully picked Christine up out of her wheelchair and carried her to me.

I took her in my arms and held her. "Christine, have you put all your heart and trust in Jesus as your savior?" A young man from the shore translated.

Christine looked at me and said, "Yes."

"My sister, I baptize you in the name of the Father, Son, and Holy Spirit. Buried with the Lord in baptism . . ."

I bent my knees. To get her fully submerged, I sank in the water to just below my mouth. Noting that she was fully under, I raised up and lifted her a little out of the water.

". . . and raised to walk in the newness of life!" I declared her faith to Christine and to the small crowd, which burst into applause. A few women trilled in celebration.

And right on cue, when we pushed into the darkness and made progress reaching unreached peoples, Ali and I would go sideways again.

THE REAL PROBLEM IN MY MARRIAGE

Ali and me with Lake Victoria in the background, 2009.

N 2008, I prayed a little prayer: "God search my heart." I was inspired by my biblical hero, David, and Psalm 139:23: "Search me, O God, and know my heart; try me and know my anxious thoughts."

It's the little prayers that get you. God was about to answer, and it was going to be brutal.

At 2:30 a.m. sometime in 2009, Ali and I were still up having an intense discussion, otherwise known as a fight. I looked at her and said, "We've been having this same fight for fourteen years. We clearly can't fix it. I think we need help."

Sometime earlier I had been eating lunch with my friend Todd Szalkowski. In the course of our discussion, he made an offhand comment about seeing a counselor with his wife. We really didn't talk any more about that. But I filed it away. I viewed Todd as a strong, impressive guy. At the time, I thought only weak people with problems saw counselors. At 2:30 a.m. I thought, "If Todd can see someone, then maybe I can too."

I had struck up a friendship with another man named Rob Sherman. We went to church together and he was a licensed professional counselor. I called him that next day for a referral for Ali and me. He said, "Why don't you come and see me. If it's not a good fit, I have plenty of counselors I can refer you to." We made an appointment.

When we entered Rob's office, my thinking was if he could help Ali, and ideally fix her, our marriage would greatly improve. About thirty or forty minutes into the first appointment, Rob looked right at me and said, "Mike, you are emotionally [slow]." He actually used a non-PC word that he later regretted, but it was one hundred percent accurate.

I felt like he hit me with a sledgehammer but here's how right he was. It took me about a year to figure out what he even meant by me being "emotionally slow." I was significantly disconnected from my feelings. Rob was the perfect counselor for us, and particularly for me. He would argue and fight with me. He knew I was a challenger, and he rose to challenge me. He knew I needed those healthy confrontations to hear him, and to hear Ali.

He told us, "You guys have a good marriage. If you do nothing, you can muddle through and keep a pretty good marriage. But if you do the work, you can have a much better marriage." I was about to find out what "doing the work" meant. I also deeply wanted a great marriage. I felt I couldn't accept mediocrity. Ali and I threw ourselves into the emotional work in a serious way. Rob was generous with his time, particularly with me. In addition to being disconnected from my feelings, I had strength and weakness upside down. I was deeply insecure, and I had trust, fear, and control issues. Facing those, admitting those, and then leaning into them—their roots and their effects on others in my life—was deeply painful. It was also embarrassing. I was a ministry leader who was a mess. I felt shame and embarrassment over the four horses of my apocalypse: insecurity, fear, control, and trust.

The best way I can describe the process Rob put Ali and me through is like this. Imagine you have old, deep wounds on your physical body. They've scarred over, but they didn't heal right, so they're still painful, and maybe even ooze from time to time. To heal properly, you have to burn off and cut out the scar tissue, then dig beneath it and clean out the substances causing the pain and infection. Only then can you heal properly, and you're still going to have a scar.

Ali and I, with Rob's help, brought up and out all the ugly, painful, embarrassing, and hurtful things in our lives and marriage. Instead of avoiding them, we faced them. We asked God to help us heal properly, and we decided to fight for one another. There were stretches in the next three years—three long years—where we hurt one another even more, didn't particularly like one another, and sometimes got less healthy and more ugly as we learned how to *get* healthy and love one another well. From the beginning of our marriage, we took divorce off the table. We didn't, and still don't, even joke about it. That forced us to fight and work through our junk.

After about a year with Rob, he graduated us. He told us we had the tools, awareness, and a new way of thinking. Now, we needed to keep using these tools and keep working. Ali felt like now that she had identified some specific issues she was facing, she needed more work. She joined Celebrate Recovery (CR) at our church. Saddleback Church created CR in 1991. It is a Christ-based twelve-step recovery program to help anyone with a hurt, hang-up, or habit you struggle with. I needed a break. I was exhausted from my work with Rob and had no intention of going to CR.

In CR, the fourth step is considered the most difficult. It's on this step you list out those hurts, hang-ups, and habits. You do a "fearless moral inventory."[6] You literally write out the worst things that you've done or have had perpetrated upon you. This is where your sponsor helps you see patterns and blind spots you probably weren't aware of. This is also where you see who you'll need to make amends to later on in the process. It's deeply personal.

Let me pause here to tell you of a moment I had in my office in this same time period. Missy Williams (of Seed Effect) and I were talking about CR and the pros and cons of these types of programs. Suddenly, she stood up, and I'm pretty sure she pointed her finger at me. She said, "You'll never be the leader you could be if you don't go to CR."

I considered what she said, but I didn't want to take her advice. I thought, *I'm a ministry leader. Ministry leaders don't go to Celebrate Recovery. That's for people with problems.*

My biggest problem was my insecurity. What had Ali written down in her fearless moral inventory? My insecurity wanted to know. I felt I had to know. I felt somewhere in that inventory was the other shoe she was going to drop on me. She communicated that when she was

---

6 "The 12 Steps and Their Biblical Comparisons," Celebrate Recovery, https://celebraterecovery.efree.org/home/the-12-steps.

further in her process, she'd sit me down and share it with me on her terms. Not good enough for me.

I took matters into my own hands and read it without her permission.

My Slice of Humble Pie

I called Rob and talked with him about what I had done. Two things were clear. One, I needed to tell Ali, and two, I was a slave to my insecurity. I had violated her. It was time to eat another, huge piece of humble pie and face those four horsemen anew: insecurity, fear, control, and trust.

I drove to David and Missy's house and told them that they were right and that I needed to go to CR. I told them I would find a church where they offered it. Missy again spoke directly to me. "That's part of your issue. You need to do this at your home church."

Ugh.

Our church hosted CR on Thursday nights. I rode there with Ali. I felt like I was going to die. The doors to the church felt like a thousand pounds each. I couldn't believe I was actually going to a twelve-step recovery group. I was totally humiliated. On top of my humiliation, I would have to see the ladies in Ali's particular twelve-step study group. They all knew what I had done. So I had that to look forward to. Further, I felt beyond pathetic coming to the group with my issue as insecurity.

After the mixed group, I went to the men's open group. You stay in open group until you have enough men to form a step study group where you work through the twelve steps. God gave me the most wonderful facilitator who instantly made me feel comfortable. In open group, you can say anything you want so long as you don't offend your fellow members. No one can respond to you. That's called crosstalk, and it's not allowed. For weeks, I would introduce myself. "Hi, I'm Mike and I'm a grateful believer in recovery for insecurity, fear, control, and trust." Then for those same weeks, I would follow that with, "I hate being here." Every week I only said that I hated being there, but I kept showing up. A young guy in open group, who would go on to do the step study with me, started stifling a laugh because I'd say I hated being there, every week.

One Thursday, I walked in late to the mixed group time where we would all, men and women, worship together and hear a testimony or learn a step. I stopped in the back and looked around as they sang and worshiped. It was a cross-section of humanity. White-collar to homeless and everyone in between.

In that moment, CR radically changed for me. I thought this was one of the most beautiful expressions of church I'd ever experienced. Each of us in that room was there because we knew we didn't have what it takes. We'd accepted that unless Jesus (step 3) comes through for us, we're hopeless. We're bound to those hurts, habits, and hang-ups, and life would forever be unmanageable. It was beautiful. My attitude totally changed.

To wrap this story up, I worked the steps. My testimony is that it felt like a miracle to me. Jesus met me afresh in the process. I entered with thoughts and hang-ups that I thought I could never get past. Somehow, miraculously, God took them away. I still struggle, I still feel things, but I feel like an almost completely different person. Missy was right. I am a better leader, but more importantly I'm a better husband, dad, and friend. Ali and I now like to share our story and pray often that God will use it to help others struggling in their marriage.

God searched my heart. It was rough, ugly, and hard. But he didn't leave me there. He walked with me through it, and ultimately healed me. He's amazing.

God Can Use Anyone, But . . .

Clearly this is a big theme, and I'm a huge beneficiary of God's grace. But, if you feel called to missions, please do a serious self-examination first. And I challenge you to ask for feedback from people who will be brutally honest with you. I like Harvard professor Sheila Heen's advice when asking for feedback: What's one thing I'm doing well? And, what's one thing I need to hear or improve?[7] Don't be defensive with what you hear. Consider it.

In my missional context, I've observed some missionaries who are working out their pathology on the local population. They've run *from* something at home rather than *to* God's calling. Which are you?

The barriers to entry in the developing world are often too low. It's simply too easy to set up ministry shop in many of these communities. Communities where the cultural default setting is hospitality and, in East Africa, to appear to agree regardless of how they actually feel because they prioritize relationship. We need better filters to protect the already poor and vulnerable from the well-meaning but misguided missionary. Take your flaws to Jesus. Before you go to the field, work on them, with Jesus, first.

---

7 "How to Use Others' Feedback to Learn and Grow | Sheila Heen | TEDxAmoskeagMillyardWomen," posted June 22, 2015, by TEDx Talks, YouTube, https://www.youtube.com/watch?v=FQNbaKkYk_Q.

PART 3

EMPOWER ONE

THE DIFFICULT ORIGIN STORY OF EMPOWER ONE

'M GOING TO try and thread a needle in this chapter, and I hope I don't stick my finger and bleed.

I love e3. The fingerprints of my mentors from my time there are everywhere at Empower One. They are a fantastic church-planting and disciple-making movement ministry. I want to honor them and be godly in my words. At the same time, I want to be honest that during the end of my tenure, there was a struggle for organizational health—one I'm happy to say they've recovered from as of this writing.

When Ali and I went to counseling with Rob, he said, "Often, unhealthy people are drawn to helping professions. Like ministry, social work, even things like police work." Because of this, some ministries experience seasons of unhealth, or worse. One of the audiences I hope reads this book are my peers in ministry. I want you to know you're not crazy or alone if you find yourself in an unhealthy environment.

I own my part in not leaving e3 as well as I should have. There are places I failed, and my warts showed a bit too brightly. And, as you'll see later, I'm not throwing rocks from my glass house. Five years after we left e3 and started Empower One, I looked at my own team and named our unhealth. Then I had to face the fact that our unhealth was my fault.

But in August of 2012, I had to face the truth that God was leading me away from e3.

Our Season Is Over

"Our season here is over. Your season may not be, but ours is over," Ali told the Sudan team.

I had gathered the Sudan team for a two-day working retreat. Ali and I had decided that our season at e3 was over, and it was time for me to depart. I was so worried that I would be accused of recruiting the team to leave with me, that whatever I said prior to Ali's quote above made no sense. I don't even remember what I said. I just remember looking out over the faces in front of me and seeing question marks form over everyone's heads.

I had also just made a big mistake.

I was informing my team before I had informed my leadership. At that moment, I justified it because trust between leadership and me had eroded. Regardless, I was wrong. Worse, one of the team members was also a member of the board. My action, or lack thereof, put him in a bad spot. He was obligated to call the CEO. The next day, I was asked to come to a meeting with the leadership team.

The Terrible Meeting Before the Other Terrible Meeting

A few weeks prior to that fateful night, I was sitting in a small conference room with my CEO. I had asked for a private meeting to share some concerns with him. I knew of his love for the Army, so I couched the meeting as a noncommissioned officer letting the top general know how the troops were feeling. What they were feeling was disconnected, overlooked, and that we were operating in unhealthy silos.

When I finished talking, I noted that his face was bright red. *Oh no, I've screwed up,* I thought.

"I've heard these same things before," he started. "I've heard them from . . ." And he listed four guys who had all committed major moral failures, one leading to prison.

Now *I* turned red and noticed my breathing was fast. All I could think about was how badly I needed to get out of that room. I tried to say as little as possible and just leave. His implication was crystal clear: By bringing my critique I was hiding a secret life of sin. (I wasn't.) I was devastated, and it was an emotional drive home that day.

I felt this incredible calling to Sudan and South Sudan. I felt an obligation to David Kaya and my team, and yet I knew I needed to leave this leadership team. I resolved to slink back to my office and team, keep my head down, and wait for an opportunity to go.

During this time period, a donor at e3 gave a gift earmarked for developing young leaders. I was invited to the group despite not being exactly young anymore. John Townsend, coauthor of the book *Boundaries*, led our sessions. Several other participants shared frustrations at the unhealthy environment. I determined to say and share nothing in the group. Now that I knew what my leadership thought of me, I knew the last thing I should do is say anything more.

I pulled John Townsend aside one day during a break. I shared with him my interaction with my CEO. He crossed his arms, exhaled through his teeth, and said, "Well, you're going to have to decide if you can live with this or not." And then he affirmed the lack of organizational health.

His comment felt like permission to go. I resolved to leave.

I heard about another small ministry that was looking for an executive director. They worked in Uganda and the Dominican Republic. I applied for the job. My thought was maybe I could sway them to South Sudan. In hindsight, this entire dalliance with them was foolish of me. Ali and I interviewed with the board of that Uganda/DR ministry, and I accepted their executive director position.

It just so happened this was the same week I was hosting the e3 Sudan team's meeting noted above.

Now it was time for me to meet with e3's leadership team and do what I should have done much earlier: talk about leaving.

The Origin Story Gets Messier

It was one of the worst meetings of my life. I braced myself, received my shots, and got called at least one name: One of the leaders compared me to the disciple from Iscariot. I think I took them by surprise when I was meek and indicated I wouldn't ask anyone on the team to come with me, and I had no plan to take any money or assets with me. I held to that. I told every member of my team to make a decision that was best for them. I even told David Kaya that I was fine if he wanted to stay. I meant it.

While the leadership team worked through what to do, I met with the interim leader of the Uganda/DR ministry to begin to get oriented and learn about the job.

I sat across from her at her desk. I had my notebook out. Within thirty seconds of sitting across from her, I knew I'd made a horrible mistake. I felt sick and nervous. I had no passion for where they were working or what they were doing. My calling was for the unreached in Sudan and South Sudan. My idea that I could sway them to move to Sudan and South Sudan was disrespectful, foolish, and prideful.

I drove to a taco restaurant, sat at a table alone, and thought, *Am I going crazy? What is wrong with me? I've quit my job. I can't take this new job with integrity. What on earth should I do?* I prayed and stared out at the cars whizzing by. *Call Tim.* I felt like I should call Tim.

Tim was a longtime supporter. Ali and I loved spending time with him and his wife. I gave him a very high-level explanation of my situation, then asked, "Tim, what if I started a new ministry, but working in the same place, doing the same work?"

Tim replied, "Mike, Judy and I support the work God has you doing. We think the world of Ali. We'd be supportive of you guys. It might be time to start something new." For clarity, I called for his advice, not financial support. I was still resolved not to recruit anyone, staff or donors, to what I was doing.

Sitting in that taco place, I decided to launch a new ministry: Empower Sudan. This was our original name. More on that in a bit.

I reached out to the Uganda/DR ministry board chairman and asked to meet with him in person. I drove to his house. He walked me to his back porch. We sat down. I said, "I am so sorry. I'm embarrassed, and I'm so sorry to put you and the board through this, but I can't accept this position. I am called to South Sudan and Sudan, and I won't serve you well."

I don't recall his words, but his grace and graciousness toward me is burned into me. He had every right to be angry, and he'd have been in the right to accuse me of being wishy-washy. Instead, he was so kind. We agreed that I should call each board member and explain my heart and decision. I felt like they deserved at least that from me. To a person, they were gracious and kind.

e3 had assigned a vice president to handle my exit. I let him know I was going to start a new ministry called Empower Sudan. After a week of him taking a deep dive into e3's South Sudan's operations, he learned we had over forty Africans on staff, a Bible School, multiple primary schools, three vehicles, $1 million of gross revenue coming in, and more.

I don't know e3's motivation, but I've assumed they didn't want the upkeep for those ministry expenses. Plus, they were operating a different ministry model that had almost no on-the-field personnel and overhead. He called me and said they'd transfer all the field assets to Empower Sudan, and that I was free to go and communicate with any donor who had been supporting the Sudan work. Then, they talked with David Kaya and each American team member, asking if he or she wanted to stay or leave. Four American team members joined me, David Kaya took the leap, and a few stayed.

I was both scared and energized.

I didn't know what to do. A colleague referred me to an accountant in Austin who specialized in nonprofits. He became a godsend. He pointed me to Form 1023, which led to our 501(c)(3). The same lawyer who had also helped start a clean water ministry, and who is like a brother to me, walked me through that 1023 process and provided a set of bylaws I edited for a board I also had to put together.

Seed Effect had left e3 a few months earlier, and their operations director pointed me in the right direction for software to accept donations. Our new accountant said he'd never had a client work as fast as we did. He probably didn't have one as filled with fear as I was. Within six weeks, we were up and running, accepting donations, and moving forward. David Kaya had prepared the team in Africa to live on nothing for a short season, but God provided for all of us. No one missed a paycheck.

I should have handled how I left e3 differently. I own that. But starting Empower Sudan/One was the right move. It's given me more grace for some degree of mess in churches and ministries. God was, and remains, far more gracious than we deserve. It was painful. My great friend, Todd Szalkowski, went to bat for me, unasked by me and unknown by me. As a result, he departed e3 four months later and would join us the next year. I counted three e3 board members as friends. I went to church with one. The one I went to church with let me know he was angry with me, but we talked about it and kept our relationship. The other two never talked with me again. One member of e3's leadership suggested I was breaking a glass sculpture that could never be put back together and worried I was involved in a deep, hidden sin. That stuff really hurt. I'm sure I hurt them too.

Years later, the board of e3 totally changed the leadership team. I'm friends with the person they installed as the interim CEO, and I unreservedly endorse e3 as a great ministry today.

Different Name, Same Mission

So why is our ministry now called Empower One rather than Empower Sudan? When David and I started working together, Sudan was one country. In that spirit, we wanted our name to be Empower Sudan. The problem was, until 2018, Sudan was on the United States' State Sponsors of Terrorism list along with North Korea, Iran, Cuba, and Syria. Every time we wired money, the government froze the wire. I had to call the bank and personally guarantee we were not funding terrorism and that I was not actually sending the money to the country of Sudan. (We weren't, by the way.) I anticipated this issue, which is why our legal name is Cush Empowerment Group. Empower Sudan and Empower One are both d/b/a names.

One and a half years after leaving e3 and starting Empower Sudan, we renamed and rebranded the ministry. I was filled with fear, again. I thought we'd be perceived as wishy-washy and unreliable. The exact opposite happened. When we unveiled the new Empower One name and look, it shot a jolt of electricity through the ministry.

God kept being good to us.

WAR UP CLOSE

THOUSAND-YARD STARES.

James Abwong and Peter Mayik had them. In late 2013, they sat near one another on a set of stairs leading to a small, two-room concrete house in the middle of our church compound in Nimule, South Sudan. They seemed to hold a deep connection that comes from sharing an intensely traumatic experience. It had been over a month since they'd run from their homes in the dark while bullets whizzed by their heads. I had flown over to see them and to be with them, practicing the ministry of presence. I wanted our friends and partners to know we were with them and wouldn't abandon them in their darkest hour. I stood by Peter and James, and they were still visibly in shock. It was as if they did everything in slow motion. They moved slowly, talked slowly, thought slowly. They had two bedrolls in one of the rooms and all of their belongings in bags lying nearby.

James and Peter had been in a village in the northeast part of South Sudan called Baliet, a small village on the bank of the Sobat

River, which feeds into the Nile on its journey north to Egypt. Baliet is the same village where we put the Christian school, which changed the community. It's a place that reminds me of western Kansas because it's flat with scrub trees here and there. It's fantastic land for grazing cattle and growing sorghum. It's the home of our regional leader, John Monychol. From Baliet, John, James, and Peter, along with a few other leaders, had started planting churches throughout the region and had set up an extension center of NEATS.

From a church-planting perspective, Baliet's location is strategic. It's almost exactly between the capital city of Malakal, which lies to its west and sits on the Nile, and Nasir, a significant city near the border of Ethiopia to its east. What's even more strategic is that, generally speaking, everything west of Baliet is populated by the Dinka tribe, South Sudan's largest and most dominant tribe. Everything east is populated by the Nuer tribe, South Sudan's second-largest tribe. But what was strategic for church planting became a nightmare for Baliet.

Through their thousand-yard stares, Peter and James recounted the nightmare to me.

"It was the middle of the night," Peter told me. "I heard the crack of gunfire, and I saw men moving from the river. I told my wife to pack one bag quickly, and I woke my children. We only had time to pack one bag. We began to run into the bush."

The Dinka and the Nuer had started fighting a few weeks earlier, sparked by the alleged assassination attempt on South Sudan's president, Salva Kiir.

That night, the warring tribes were meeting in the middle: Baliet.

John Monychol

John baptizing a new believer in the Sobat River in South Sudan.

I need to pause here and tell you about John Monychol, because he played a massive role in Peter's family's escape. John had run from Baliet before, but it was in the 1980s, during the previous civil war. When war came to Baliet back then, he and his family ran east into Ethiopia, where the United Nations had set up refugee camps.

What John didn't know was that the SPLA controlled these camps, and they were hungry for recruits. Every young male they could find, they conscripted into their army. At only eleven years old, John found himself drafted into the rebel army.

When he recounted his story to me, John said, "I could not even carry a gun. I was too weak, so at first I just helped the other soldiers."

John grew strong enough to carry a gun and engage in warfare, and he learned how to live off the land to survive, including pillaging villages—something he's not proud of today. When John was nineteen, he was in a fierce firefight with the Sudanese Army in his home state of Upper Nile. The fight was going badly, and his unit was losing. Men fell all around him. Moving positions, he felt a sting near his right ankle. Looking down, he saw he'd been shot and was bleeding.

He made both a genius and a horrific quick decision. Seeing a pile of dead bodies nearby, he laid among them and played dead. Terrified of being discovered and not knowing if the enemy army was still nearby, he kept his position for three days. Finally, he heard a helicopter. Looking up, he saw a bright red cross on its door.

The Red Cross found him, bandaged his leg, rehydrated him, then flew him to the Kakuma refugee camp in northwest Kenya. In Kakuma he found Jesus, and God transformed his life. He attended seminary in Nairobi, but as soon as the fighting cooled down in South Sudan, he returned to his home village.

I met John in 2007 at a small meeting for pastors. He stood out, and we started officially working together in 2010.

Running From Gunfire

On the night that the civil war was coming to Baliet, John's military experience kicked in. He quickly discerned where the threat was coming from. He not only gathered his own family but most of the villagers and directed them north. He knew that if they could get to Paloich, it had an airstrip. It was also a significant oil field, so it was heavily guarded by the government. Neither the Dinka nor the Nuer would engage there. Hundreds of people, carrying at most one bag, and many with nothing, followed John on the ninety-one-mile walk through the bush from Baliet to Paloich.

Peter's wife was almost nine months pregnant the night they ran. The trauma and the running through the bush cost them their baby's life. While Peter recounted their experience to me, he relayed that his wife was still in a hospital in Juba, the capital. She would never be able to have children again. For any woman, this is devastating. For a South Sudanese woman, it's compounded by the cultural expectation to produce many children.

James had started with John and the group, but after walking north, he directed his family west toward Malakal. The UN quickly established a camp just north of the airport. James registered his family, set up a tarp for a temporary home, and waited.

The food rations were not enough for James and his family. They were getting hungry, and the kids were upset. While not a doctor, James had extensive medical training and often worked for medical NGOs in the Upper Nile. A wonderful American doctor had taken a liking to James. When the American doc would conduct medical clinics to bolster our work in the community, James would assist him. He loaded an iPad with tons of medical information to help James and had given it to James as a gift.

James walked out of the camp with his iPad. He found a man in town who bought it from him. He took that cash, bought food for his family, and secured their places on a relief plane from there to Juba. From Juba, Empower One helped them get to Nimule.

John was in Nimule with James and Peter as well. He was handling his shock and trauma differently. He was in action mode. We turned our church compound in Nimule into a way station for refugees. They would flee the Upper Nile and get to the capital city of Juba. From there, we would arrange transport for our church members and anyone else we could to Nimule. At the church compound, they would gather themselves, eat, and rest. From Nimule, they would cross into Uganda and register with the UN. The UN would then assign them to a refugee camp, and they would rebuild their lives on a thirty-by-thirty-meter plot. John was directing most of this traffic.

In a quiet moment, he asked me for advice. "My children are having very bad dreams. They saw a lot of dead bodies. My daughter even had to step over a dead body. What can I do to help them?"

My meager, inadequate response was, "Let them talk about everything, and let them talk together, with you." We had a counselor on staff at the time who was training to specialize in trauma, and I told John we would get her involved. I was out of my depth. But I could buy food, help with transportation, and keep practicing the ministry of presence.

As tough as John is—and he is a tough, strong Dinka—his pastor's heart is tender.

"My brother, there was a young girl who died in the bush while we were walking."

I listened closely.

"We were walking, and there were some vehicles that had broken down. Maybe from some time ago. This girl, she was thirsty. We were all thirsty. No one saw her walk to those vehicles. There was battery acid. It looked like water to this girl. She drank it and she died. The mother was very upset. We were all very upset."

I sensed this child's death shook John more than the others he'd just witnessed.

As I stood in the church compound, I knew it was time to hit pause on our church-planting work. We would need to serve and care for refugees.

THE PIVOT

*A young boy smiles from his temporary tent home
in a refugee camp in northern Uganda.*

WE FOLLOWED JOHN, Peter, and James into the refugee
camps. For the next seven and a half years, most of our
work would be in these camps.

In Uganda, they're actually called settlements instead of camps. Uganda handles refugees about as gracefully and with as much dignity as anywhere in the world. Perhaps because they have suffered as refugees, there's more kindness. That's not to say you want to live in a settlement, but Uganda is different from almost any other country with its refugee approach. Their settlements are open, meaning the refugees are free to come and go. Refugees can work in Uganda, if they can find a job, and Uganda has a path to citizenship for refugees. Despite this distinction, I'm going to refer to them as camps. One, because it's more familiar nomenclature for you, and two, it's what the refugees call them.

John and the people from the Upper Nile were the first wave into Uganda. Other tribes joined Riek Machar's rebellion against the government, and fighting spread throughout the southern states of South Sudan. By 2016, 1.5 million South Sudanese would move into twenty-three refugee camps strung across northwest Uganda. That same year, one camp, Bidi Bidi, became the largest refugee camp on earth when it swelled to almost three hundred thousand refugees.

Yomima's story illustrates a later wave who entered the camps after John's people. She was the women's ministry leader at our church in Nimule and served as a wildlife ranger with the rank of sergeant in charge of communications for the Nimule National Park.

In a 2016 interview we filmed of Yomima's experience, she said, "Because I am a wildlife ranger, at any time [the government] can tell us, 'Okay, from here you go' because you are able to carry a gun and fight. . . . But then how will I be able to take care of the children? And how will the future of these children be?"[8]

Gunmen came through her neighborhood one night, kicking in doors, looting, and shooting a few resistors. She had been spared,

---

8 "Yomima HQ," posted November 15, 2016, by Empower One, YouTube, https://www.youtube.com/watch?v=DjNOgbFI9l8.

but it was enough for her. She chose her family over her career and decided to head for the camps in Uganda.

In our video, she continued, "I have three children, they are all girls. I also have two orphans. I have my cousins' sisters and my brother's [children]. We are all in total, nineteen."

Yomima recounted the journey from Nimule to the camps, sitting safely in her doorway in Pagirinya refugee camp. The setting sun lit up one side of her face while she shared, and it cast a soft light on the mud-packed wall behind her.

"That's why it has moved me to come to Uganda. During when we were coming, you know, we walked. We slept outside. We were washed by rain. And the following day they told us we would have to go, and the compound was full of people. There was one woman whose child fell from her hand. And people stepped on that child. And that child died."

This compound Yomima refers to was the intake center for freshly arriving refugees.

"Police began to cane people until one woman, an old mama, passed away also in that place. We spent two days in that place. There was no water. That day I cried with tears because of what happened. Then we really struggled talking with [the children]. Telling them we should be patient. You know patience pays—you just have to wait for what God will do for us."

Yomima displayed incredible resolve, keeping all nineteen kids in her traveling party together and their spirits up enough to keep going. Yomima also represents the vast majority of fleeing refugees: women. The strength these women displayed is inspiring. And while Yomima was spared sexual violence, many women were not. A United Nations press release from October 2014 reads, "In a press conference today at UN Headquarters following her first mission to South Sudan to assess the situation of sexual violence in conflict in the country, Ms. Bangura [the UN Special Representative of the Secretary-General on Sexual Violence in Conflict] explained that in her 30 years of experience she had never seen anything like what she witnessed in the northern town of Bentiu, where hundreds of civilians were massacred in April of this year and many more were raped."[9]

After those two terrible days, Yomima registered all nineteen of her party with the UN and Uganda. They assigned her a small plot of land. She received a few tarps to provide her with an immediate shelter, a few blankets, cooking oil, beans, flour, and a small amount of sugar. The aid worker encouraged her to quickly build a tukul and plant a garden to help sustain her family. Yomima loaded her group into a large truck and headed to her temporary home.

Yomima wrapped up her interview with us by saying, "The good thing I am giving thanks to the Lord for what he has done. I go to [the Bible] talking that those who believe in Jesus, he will send his people to care for them and take care of them. Pastor David, he decided to help me."

A Refugee Ministry

David did help her and many others. Empower One pivoted to a refugee ministry. It continued our pattern of simply responding to what was in front of us. When we couldn't find qualified leaders, we started NEATS. When communities where we started churches had no schools, we started small schools. Our friends had to run away from their homes and live in refugee camps in northern Uganda. So we decided, *Let's follow them and figure out what God wants us to do.* We didn't lose sight of our mission to reach unreached tribes and plant churches, but God's second greatest command

9 "South Sudan at 'Crossroads' as It Seeks to Combat Sexual Violence, Says UN Official," United Nations, October 20, 2014, https://news.un.org/en/story/2014/10/481502.

is to love your neighbor. Our neighbors had lost everything. We needed to help.

Seeing your friends and ministry partners lose everything and have to move into a refugee camp is both devastating and overwhelming. Compared with the United Nations, USAID, Oxfam, World Vision International, or Samaritan's Purse, Empower One was tiny. We were trying to make sure all our African staff got paid, and we were raising funds for outreaches and missions. We had no ability to meet the scale of refugees.

Once again, the American team and I had to lean heavily on our African teammates. For the next few years, we would share what resources we could provide and rely on our local leaders to divvy them up best. I had to fully adopt the starfish story, which was adapted from Loren Eiseley's "The Star Thrower" essay:[10]

"A young girl was walking along a beach upon which thousands of starfish had been washed up during a terrible storm. When she came to each starfish, she would pick it up and throw it back into the ocean. People watched her with amusement.

"She had been doing this for some time when a man approached her and said, 'Little girl, why are you doing this? Look at this beach! You can't save all these starfish. You can't begin to make a difference!'

"The girl seemed crushed, suddenly deflated. But after a few moments, she bent down, picked up another starfish, and hurled it as far as she could into the ocean. Then she looked up at the man and replied, 'Well, I made a difference for that one!'"

David Kaya again proved to be God's perfect partner for me. Having grown up in refugee camps, he quickly shifted into a proactive gear and came up with a plan to make a difference for those we could while in exile.

---

10 "The Tale of the Starfish," The Starfish Foundation, https://www.thestarfish-change.org/starfish-tale.

DAVID LEADS THROUGH WAR

WHEN WE MADE Kajo Keji our headquarters in 2006, I was disappointed. I felt it was too far south, away from the more unreached areas. After a few years, I changed my mind completely. I thought its location actually made it a safe haven from the more aggressive tribes in other parts of the country.

Turns out, I was wrong. Everything changed in December of 2016.

By this point in the war, multiple militias that opposed the government had formed near our headquarters. The army came to confront them. We had to evacuate. David flew into action. We used our flatbed lorry and our Land Cruisers. We packed them with people and ferried them to Uganda to safety. We kept crossing the border back and forth until it was finally too unsafe.

A Moment of Levity

Because you have to find humor in terrible situations, here's one funny note. When we returned to Kajo Keji five years later, we found that rebels and soldiers had pulled all the metal doors and windows out of our buildings. They'd cut the metal poles holding up our porches, and they'd pulled the electrical wire out of our walls. They sold the metal in Uganda. In the chaos of fleeing, we left most of our more dense theology books in our small library.

They were untouched.

You Can Be Sad Later

"Come to the office in Arua."

David sent this simple message to pastors who were having to leave their homes and churches because of the expansion of the war. Six months earlier, we rented a compound in Arua, Uganda, a large city in the northwest corner of Uganda. From Arua, we could access many of the refugee camps. It also had a good airport, and it was close enough to the border to be a safe haven if one had to flee South Sudan. David gathered every pastor he could from the affected areas and brought them to our compound.

He told them, "You will stay here for three weeks. We have cooks, and they will cook you good food. We are bringing you meat. You just rest, brothers. I want you to just rest, eat well, and sing and worship together."

Then David answered the question forming in all their minds: *Why are we here?*

"After these three weeks, you will have no rest. I am sending you into the camps. You will start new churches throughout the camps.

You will bring comfort to these people. You will totally empty yourself out. So these three weeks, you must rest and charge your battery!"

The pastors were solemn. There was gratitude for the respite and sanctuary of our safehouse and now temporary headquarters. The rest was deeply needed. But their minds leaped to the task David was calling them to, and they felt its gravity.

David had anticipated the expansion of war. He'd also grown up in these same camps now swelling with refugees. He switched from reactive to proactive: Let's start or reconstitute our churches in these camps and be beacons of light, comfort, and hope.

"We are buying many hoes, shovels, and even pickaxes. We are also buying seeds. Brothers, do not think you will be in these camps for a short time. Get your mind to accept you will be in these camps for years! We must encourage the people to start their gardens."

David did not believe the food rations provided by the United Nations, Uganda, and NGOs would be sufficient. He remembered his own hunger.

"You tell your people to go outside of the camp. Make peace with the local people. You help them negotiate so they can cultivate much larger gardens."

This was a significant strategy David believed in deeply. The government established these camps in the bush. Most were forty-five-minute drives, at minimum, to a major town. There was plenty of fertile land surrounding these camps. David knew they could work deals out with the locals and establish far larger gardens than their small camp plots allowed.

"Empower One is not the United Nations. We are not Lutheran World Relief, brothers. We do not have these big resources. However, if you have a family that is really hungry and struggling, you call my phone. We have some little food, we will give you food secretly to you so you do not have problems with the community overrunning you and your home for this food. And you can give this small food to these struggling families."

David displayed a calm strength, a great plan, and inspirational leadership.

THE UNLIKELY

ON ONE OF my visits to the refugee camps over the next three years, I spent a couple days in one of our churches preaching and encouraging the small group of believers. I pulled the pastor aside during a tea break and asked him, "If you have anyone whose testimony I should hear, would you help me meet with them?"

I wanted to gather a few stories to share with the American church when I returned. The pastor had me spend time with three of his church members. We walked across the dusty road from the church to the grounds of a primary school. We set up chairs between two buildings for a little bit of privacy. That's how I met Rebecca.

Rebecca was born and raised in the DR Congo. We sat nearly knee-to-knee between those school buildings the UN built inside the Rhino refugee camp. She graciously allowed me to record her testimony and gave me permission to share it with the American church.

"My father had five wives. I am the daughter of the first wife." Rebecca started meekly, almost in a whisper. "I only completed [sixth grade]. My father said he did not have money for school fees."

I noticed deep sadness in Rebecca's eyes as she unfolded her life story.

"I married at seventeen years. I had four children. We did not have enough money. I went by foot to a quarry nearby. I broke stones for some small money."

Having seen this often in Africa, I knew this meant she sat on the ground for hours at a time breaking stone into aggregate for construction. She broke the stones using only a small hammer.

"I became sick and I almost died. My neighbor took me to the clinic. I was very sick. The doctor told me I had diabetes. So I had to change everything about how I ate just to survive. I saw many people gathering in my town. I went to where they were. A man from Israel was preaching about Jesus Christ. I walked to the front of the crowd that day and prayed to Jesus Christ. From that day I have never had diabetes."

Rebecca was now speaking to me above a whisper. She was feeling more comfortable; she adjusted her long, teal dress and continued her story.

"I was always at the church from that day on. I began reading the Bible and I was very happy. The pastor asked a group of us to go and help another young pastor start a new church. I was excited, and of course I said yes."

Rebecca's countenance changed again. She lowered her voice again and seemed to turn inward, distant. "When I was riding a motorbike to go to the new church, rebels attacked us. They shot the motorbike driver, and they took me away with them."

Some sources estimate a mind-blowing one hundred and twenty rebel groups operate in eastern DR Congo.[11]

"The army rescued me. I knew I was pregnant, but I did not know who the father was. When I returned to my home, my husband took

---

11 "11 Killed in Rebel Attack in Northeast Congo, Official Says," Voice of America, July 16, 2023, https://www.voanews.com/a/rebel-attack-in-northeast-congo/7183176.html.

my children and sent me back to my parents. They were quite old at that time."

The rebel groups and the government's fighting now threatened Rebecca's home village. She fled to Uganda with many of the people in her village. Crossing the border, the UN directed her to the Rhino refugee camp. She now found herself separated from anyone she knew from DR Congo and was completely alone.

"I was given a plot near this church. One Sunday, I came to pray. Pastor Banja saw my condition."

At this point, Rebecca was very pregnant.

"I told pastor I was all alone, and I had no money and no family. No one to help me. Even the women here, they would not speak with me."

She was referencing the women in the camp, not the church. They had shunned and shamed her for being pregnant and abandoned by her husband.

"Pastor saw I was sleeping with only the [tarp] from the UN. He got the deacons, and they built me my home. The church took pity on me. I feel loved by the people in the church. They help me with my children."

Children, plural. Her husband tracked her down, left their children with her, and disappeared.

At the end of our time together, Rebecca asked me, "Please pray for me."

I leaned over and put my hand on her shoulder. I started to pray for her.

As I prayed, she began to heave and shudder and cry.

Far from home in a refugee camp with no one from her tribe, God put Rebecca beside our church. The family of God becoming her family. An unlikely circumstance.

God Uses Adversity to Advance the Gospel

The Mobile Evangelism Team (MET) in a refugee camp in northern Uganda.

In the New Testament, we learn that God used another unlikely circumstance to expand his kingdom with the apostle Paul. Under house arrest in Rome, Paul wrote these words to the Philippians: "Now I want you to know, brothers and sisters, that *what has happened to me has actually served to advance the gospel.* As a result, it has become clear throughout the whole palace guard and to everyone else that I am in chains for Christ. And because of my chains, most of the brothers and sisters have become confident in the Lord and dare all the more to proclaim the gospel without fear" (Phil. 1:12, New International Version, emphasis mine).

How unlikely that God would use Paul's imprisonment to "advance the gospel?" How unlikely that a war in South Sudan would serve as the catalytic event to expose and bring more people to faith in Christ than any other period of Empower One's history?

While we would never have wished this situation on anyone, it did create a huge opportunity. There were people and tribes in the camps we might never have been able to reach inside South Sudan. Because South Sudan is one of the least developed countries on earth, physically getting to these tribes is challenging and expensive. Now they were bunched together in an area of which you could drive from one side to the other in about five hours.

We decided to blitz the area with the gospel. In America, we built a campaign to raise the funds to support it. We named it "The Unlikely."

Here's how it worked:

We sent a pair of local missionaries on motorcycles to a new area within a refugee camp where we knew we wanted to plant a church. They carried a solar-powered Jesus Film projector on their backs along with a tent and supplies to live for a week. They entered the area and spent the daytime getting to know people. At night, they played the Jesus Film. They spent the following days following up with anyone who put his or her faith in Jesus.

Then, we brought the big flatbed truck, filled with even more local missionaries. Recall the roving mission teams Moses, our hero in Part 1, wanted to join one day. This was that team, with the straightforward name of the Mobile Evangelism Team. We used our large, flatbed truck that had railings and a cage for covering. We covered it with a tarp and loaded it with tents, food, cooking equipment, the Jesus Film, and a team of about twenty people. They followed the motorcycle team and lived in that area for a month. They played the Jesus Film at night and spent their time following up, starting Bible studies, and beginning to disciple new believers. We sent NEATS graduates, and they would start a church in that area for these new believers.

We ran this "Unlikely" campaign for three years: 2017 through 2019. In those three years, God helped us so that 314,596 people heard the gospel, 62,306 prayed to receive Christ, and 248 new churches were started.

God can redeem any situation.

NUMB

I N JANUARY 2017, that friend, zealous advocate, and trusted advisor Todd Szalkowski shockingly passed away at fifty-two years of age from a heart attack. Todd was the most type A person I've ever met. He had been a partner at Ernst & Young when God called him into ministry. He raised support, quit that job, and jumped in. When I started in ministry, he was my support-raising mentor. One day, I sat in his office a bit dejected. I asked him, "When you were raising support, did you ever struggle with motivation?"

He answered instantly, "No, I knew how bad I wanted to get here. I never lacked motivation."

That was Todd.

That same year, I was burning out, but I didn't know it yet. So was David. We hadn't paced ourselves and we ignored Sabbath. Since 2006, we had been pushing through starting the ministry, raising funds, staff issues, leaving e3, starting a ministry (again), navigating a war, and operating in one of the darkest, most difficult countries on earth. We were more tired than we realized.

As the year was ending, I realized that our small, American team was unhealthy, and I was going numb. At one of our team meetings,

I named our unhealth. Several team members didn't get along with one another, we had too many back-channel conversations, and we were not unified. The top leader of any organization must name reality. Everyone knows and feels reality, and if you won't name it, you lose credibility. I looked at the team and said, "We're not healthy. I don't know what to do, yet, but I'm going to fix it and we're going to get healthy."

I got in my Jeep. As I was driving home from that meeting, I ate yet another large piece of humble pie. It hit me on that drive home: *Any organization is only as healthy as its top leader. That's me. I'm the problem.* It was incredibly humbling and painful. I thought I was good at building a team, but we had serious conflict on the team, and hardly anyone was happy. I was determined to face it head-on—if I could ever feel again and have energy again.

Since I was a teenager, I've felt close to God and that I could hear his voice. I've had periods of life of not following God, but I always knew I could feel and hear him. In 2017, I couldn't feel or hear him or anything else. A friend who had experienced a similar burnout sent me an article by Carey Nieuwhof called "9 Signs You're Burning Out in Leadership."[12] I had all of them.

I scheduled a coffee with my board chair and longtime friend Alfie Pino. I told him, "Alfie, I think I need a sabbatical."

He responded exactly like I thought he would: with a large exhale. "You ministry guys and these long vacations." I love Alfie. That directness and accountability—he believed those of us in ministry should have a good work ethic—is exactly why I wanted him to chair our board.

We kept talking. Todd's death came up. I said, "I envy him. Man, he's in paradise."

Alfie looked at me sideways, "Don't you want to see your grandkids?"

---

12 Carey Nieuwhof, "9 Signs You're Burning Out in Leadership," *Carey Nieuwhof* (blog), https://careynieuwhof.com/9-signs-youre-burning-out-in-leadership/.

"They'll be fine. I think I'd rather just be with God."

Alfie shifted his countenance entirely and leaned forward, "Okay, that's it! You are going on a sabbatical immediately! When are you doing this? Next month? You need to take a break right now."

And there was Alfie's heart. He could be tough, but he was tender too. Once he glimpsed my state, he became his normal, zealous advocate for me.

David Kaya and I were cooked. David went first. He took three months off, traveling to Nigeria and southwest Uganda to turn Empower One completely off, rest, and spend time with his family.

I met with our board. I passed out the Nieuwhof article on nine signs you're burning out. "I'm all ten," I joked. "Look, I'm not about to do a line of cocaine or sleep with a prostitute, but I can't feel anything. I'm in trouble."

Nieuwhof's article was helpful because he describes how people in the secular marketplace are living in a Venn diagram. That diagram is made up of three parts, which intersect with a small circle in the middle. Those three parts are a person's spiritual, emotional, and vocational lives. For those of us in vocational ministry, it's not a Venn diagram, it's a kaleidoscope.

I said, "I'm thinking of taking nine weeks, if you all approve."

Bo Ward, a board member and someone who met David before me, leaned out of his seat and looked me in the eye. "Are you just scared to ask for twelve? You need to take twelve weeks."

The board was incredibly supportive and told me to rest and come back "a better me."

He Leads Me to Still Waters

I had no idea how to sabbatical, so I interviewed over twenty people. I synthesized the advice and decided to break my sabbatical into thirds:

Month one: Rest completely and try not to think of anything to do with Empower One.

Month two: Look back, review, and evaluate.

Month three: Look forward.

I'm in an executive director/CEO peer group. They suggested I refrain from any work. They encouraged me to only do things that gave me life. A pastor friend suggested I read Ruth Haley Barton's book *Strengthening the Soul of Your Leadership.* A friend in my small group from church suggested I spend one-on-one time with each member of my immediate family. Another friend "somehow" found out I was taking a sabbatical. I hadn't been sharing it. She offered me time with a great counselor. Alfie offered me time at his ranch.

I turned everything off: email, Slack, everything. I told the team I was going one hundred percent dark. I took my friend up on her offer and visited the counselor. I cried through the whole hour. I could barely talk. I felt like a total idiot. The counselor handed me a list of Scripture to meditate over.

Next, I took Alfie up on his offer. I took my dog and went to his ranch for a week, alone. Alfie has a vineyard on his ranch. I'd walk through the vineyard and talk with God. I enjoyed the quiet and solitude.

Next, I began to slowly read Haley Barton's book. This book and this time started my journey into spiritual formation that I draw from deeply to this day. Through those pages, I discovered Dallas Willard, who's become a hero in the faith for me.

Next, I did one-on-one trips with my family. This was a stretch financially, but to this day it's one of the best things I've ever done. I started with Ali. We went to Maine and Boston. I asked each of my kids what they wanted to do. Alexa and I drove to Colorado, toured a school, and hiked in Rocky Mountain National Park. Weston and I went to Chicago. Erin and I went to Great Wolf Lodge, an indoor water park in Dallas, where we swam from the earliest check-in time possible to the last moment before we had to leave. Having everything turned off, being away, and being singularly focused on each of them were life highlights for me.

From Haley Barton's *Strengthening the Soul of Your Leadership*, I began the spiritual practice of silence and solitude. I started with ten minutes and, over the three months, built up to over twenty minutes per session. In the fifth week, one morning I could begin to *feel* God again. It was as if I had been physically numb and that morning my arms began to tingle.

I looked back and renewed my conviction that my US team dynamic wasn't healthy. When I looked forward, I felt that it was me who was holding Empower One back from growing. I searched for reading material. I found a lot of articles of founder/CEOs, particularly in the tech space, who could not make the change from founder to a CEO who is more of a manager. I found a handful of articles that addressed this concept as it relates to senior pastors who founded a church, and I found one article in the nonprofit CEO space. The gist of the articles is that it's rare for a founder to make the curve. In the tech space, they often get fired. The famous ones are the exceptions.

I bookended my sabbatical with a second visit to the counselor. I was so happy. I felt great. I felt God had literally restored my soul. Psalm 23 had taken on a much deeper meaning. The counselor said, "You appear to be a completely different person. God has indeed restored your soul."

Now it was time for reentry.

Good thing I was restored and rested, because I was about to experience an epic shake-up.

RADICAL OBEDIENCE

I N 2017, I had hired a man as a development officer, or fundraiser. By the time I'd reemerged from sabbatical, I had effectively ceded or delegated day-to-day operations to him. As a classic founder, I'm weak in administrative, process, and system-oriented functions. I wanted to delegate those and focus on where we needed to go next as a ministry and on fundraising. But I had no idea where to go next, and our team dynamic remained unhealthy and tense. On the field in Africa, evangelism, discipleship, and church planting in the refugee camps were producing tremendous spiritual fruit, and our short-term trips surged because Uganda is an easier and more comfortable country to bring Americans to compared with South Sudan.

We changed the makeup of the American team. We lost some members and helped others find new kingdom assignments. Empower One had been flat financially, we were a refugee ministry, and we weren't having much fun. When teammates don't get along and there's friction, it's not fun. I spent the year praying and thinking I was the reason why we couldn't grow. I was the lid on the ministry. In 2019, we added Matt Jones, Kelly Pearson, and Tammy Lewis.

In September of that year I drove to Ridgecrest Baptist Church in Greenville, Texas. They were, and are, a great partner church, and they had just remodeled their sanctuary. I wanted to be there for the grand reopening. It was about a forty-five-minute drive. I turned off the radio and drove in silence and talked a little with God.

I felt an almost audible voice from God: "Your assignment is complete."

I was totally rocked.

I barely heard the sermon, and I drove in silence all the way back home. I told Ali, and then I thought to bury it until Christmas. Fall is our key fundraising season, and I had to be fully engaged. At Christmas, I looked at Ali and said, "I think I'm done." She agreed.

I had no plan. I still loved Empower One, the mission, and the work. I felt it was time to be radically obedient to what I felt the Lord had said, plus I thought Empower One needed a new and different leader, one who could build systems and processes and move us from a freewheeling founder environment to a mature organization.

In January 2020, I met with our board. I told them what I felt the Lord had said and that my assignment was complete. In a later meeting, sitting over a salmon salad, Bo challenged me.

"Are you having a midlife crisis?"

I was always grateful for Bo's willingness to challenge me. I considered it, but between hearing from God plus feeling like Empower One needed something different, I stuck to it. The board asked who might lead Empower One. I suggested the man running things day-to-day.

At the board's direction, I drove to his home and we talked about what I felt God was saying to me. He and his wife prayed for a few days, and he said he'd like to enter the process to succeed me. We had another board meeting where he essentially interviewed for the role. He left the room. The board agreed on his succeeding me; however, two board members questioned it and opposed it. For unity, they voted yes, but both resigned from the board that week.

I really had no plan other than I needed to leave. I began to think about what was next. I was oddly calm. I felt like Abraham: I'm headed to a land I can't see and don't know. I felt confident God would show me what to do. We had a trip to Africa planned for the end of February. I went on that trip with the mindset it was my goodbye trip. We weren't ready to announce anything publicly, but I knew that would be my last trip as an Empower One staffer.

I pulled two plastic chairs together and sat with David under the shade of a large mango tree. Through tears I told him, "My time is over. God told me my assignment is complete. I really feel you, and the whole ministry, need a different American partner. The ministry needs systems and processes now. It needs order and more stability. I think I'm capping our growth."

David barely responded. It was so emotional for me that I really don't recall his response, but it was minimal. He did ask me, "Please, let us keep this quiet for now." I agreed. We didn't want to unnecessarily disrupt the ministry.

The trip was focused on a large pastor's conference. We'd pulled out hundreds of pastors from the refugee camps to refresh and encourage them. When I got to preach, I felt I was saying goodbye even though I didn't say it explicitly.

My successor and I worked out a timeline, about three months, and I'd announce everything at that time.

The day before we were to fly home, news reports began emerging out of China of this virus called COVID. A week after we got home, the world locked down.

A Pandemic Descends

I was so glad we hadn't announced anything.

We decided not only to keep things quiet, but I wanted to continue to help fundraising. In March, the pandemic felt existential to us at Empower One. Africa locked down as well. Again, God used a difficult circumstance for his glory. For a time, churches could not meet. Our Bible school students, graduates, pastors, and stronger disciples turned their homes into house churches. Neighbors would bring chairs, and they'd gather together to worship. A lot of our less experienced leaders grew a ton through that experience. They got more reps teaching, preaching, and literally taking care of their neighbors. We'd emerge from COVID with even stronger, more confident church leaders.

I started looking for what was next for me. I came to our weekly Zoom calls but mostly stayed silent. I turned over all the operations and decision-making to my successor. We pushed my end date from March until the end of June. Toward the end of June, we pushed it to the end of September. I was looking to stack together three or four contract and consulting opportunities. It was going to be a leap and stretch, but, again, I felt God would meet me when I leaped. I resolved to leave on September 30. We'd pushed through COVID, but it was time to go.

In August, my successor and I both took family vacations. When he returned, he told me he couldn't lead Empower One. He was pastoring a church, and with COVID, he needed to focus on his church. As big of a loop as that threw me for, it made perfect sense and felt like the right decision for him. His church did need his full-time attention.

It was left to me to inform the board. They were kind. They asked if I could step back in until December. They were open to me leaving, but they asked if I would stay until December, and if my conviction to leave remained, they would start a search for my replacement.

I agreed. I loved Empower One, David Kaya, and the mission. I had felt I was holding the ministry back, but I didn't want it to fail, and I'd led it for so long that it was easy to step back in.

However, I felt that the team couldn't trust me. How could they? I was less than thirty days from leaving. Now I'm back?

Coming Back Different: Learning to Abide

I always imagine trust like a gas tank: slow to fill, but you can empty it in a hurry. I had to work to slowly refill the team's trust tanks. Later, two team members would tell me they had no idea who I was and that I seemed like some ghost in the background. Two of the team members attended my successor's church, and I sensed that one longtime coworker, who'd basically built our entire operation's back end, was tired of working with me. I sensed he longed for structure, processes, and a leader who wouldn't start something new until he finished the previous project.

It was now September 2020. We'd made it through the lockdowns of COVID. We were entering fall and our critical fundraising season. I had no real relationship with two team members, I felt another member had one foot out the door, and I had been mentally checked out. I thought it would be down to me and my assistant/admin, Tammy, by January or February. I thought everyone would leave and we'd have to start over. And now we had to raise the bulk of our funding for 2021.

So I immediately made a mistake. Because of course I did.

I thought if I "reappeared" with a lot of confidence and a strong sense of direction, it would mitigate the team's apprehensions. It would instill confidence that I was willing to step back in and lead. I announced we would be getting back to pursuing unreached and unengaged tribes in Sudan and South Sudan.

It backfired.

I came on too strong. It shook them, and they feared I would get back to moving too fast and ignore or disrupt their current work and projects.

I dialed back. One day, I shut everything off and went for a walk at a lake near my house. Since sabbatical, I was applying my spiritual formation learnings and practices. I was trying once again, as Dallas Willard says to, "live as [Jesus's] apprentice."[13] One of these practices had become going to the lake and praying.

I came back to the team and tried again. I apologized and promised to slow down and listen to them. Then I shared what I felt our fall fundraising plan should be. "I want our fundraising plan to be simply praying and abiding in Christ. To sit in John 15. We still need to send out an end-of-year letter, emails, and try to meet with folks. We'll still do stuff, but I'm done striving or coming up with some cool strategy."

We'd pray a lot and try to learn how to "do" and how to abide. At first, doing and abiding felt like tension and opposites we were trying to bring together. The tension prompted us to pray more.

Every day I felt better and better about being back at the helm of the American side of Empower One. One day, Ali and I went to lunch with David and Missy. We were processing what had happened. Missy looked at me and said, "I'm no prophet, but I think what God meant when you heard 'Your assignment is complete' is that Empower One's time as a refugee ministry needs to close and it's time for you to get back to pursuing unreached tribes and people groups."

That resonated, and while I needed to take it slow with the team, rebuild trust, and listen, this is what was burning in my heart: It was high time to get back to going after those who've never heard Jesus's name in Sudan, South Sudan, DR Congo, Chad, and maybe more places.

---

13 "The Disappearance of Moral Knowledge in the 20th Century," Dallas Willard Ministries, https://dwillard.org/resources/articles/the-disappearance-of-moral-knowledge-in-the-20th-century.

My longtime coworker did end up also leaving Empower One to join my former successor at his church.

After that, I called Matt Jones, a member of that church, and said, "Hey man, I totally understand if you want to leave. But would you please just tell me? I'm not upset with you, and I'll actually help you, but I really don't want to be surprised."

He replied, "Mike, as long as David Kaya is leading Africa, I'm here. I'm not looking to leave. In fact, I'll do whatever you need to get through this."

That was exactly what I needed to hear.

Today, he's leading the US side of NEATS. Kelly increased her hours and took on all of our operations. We were small, but everyone stepped up, plugged holes, figured things out, and helped one another.

And we started laughing. God kept encouraging us. We had a great end of year. We'd survived, we were learning how to do ministry and life through abiding in Christ, and we had the resources to start 2021.

Good thing, because God was about to wrestle with David Kaya and impress upon him the need for flagship churches in Sudan.

THE ORIGINAL FLAGSHIP CHURCH

*David standing in front of the original flagship
church in Kajo Keji, South Sudan.*

N 2002, THE front line in the fighting in Sudan had moved north. David's home, Kajo Keji in the far south of Sudan, was peaceful again. He wanted to return home, and Harold and Beverly's time in Uganda was winding down.

One of Harold's final admonitions to David was the concept of a flagship church. David had started and strengthened churches in northern Uganda and now had moved home to Kajo Keji. Harold scraped together $10,000 and told David to build a flagship church in Kajo Keji. Harold taught David that he'd need to establish these flagship churches in key towns. They would be big enough to support their pastors and send missionaries out themselves. They would oversee the network of churches they would plant in their areas and ensure they were healthy, growing, and even multiplying. This is how the Baptists in America started, and it was the strategy they had used to grow all over America. (That's why you'll see the name "First Baptist" in American towns. These were almost always established in county seats, were first, and oversaw the planting and care of churches in their county.) Harold, no doubt, adapted this into the flagship strategy he taught David.

With Harold's help with funding, David took his advice, acquired a large piece of land, and built a church in Kajo Keji in 2002. While it can comfortably hold about two hundred and fifty people, by 2016, it would swell to over five hundred on a Sunday morning. From 2003 until the war came in 2016, David not only built the first flagship church but also installed nursery, primary, and secondary schools on the grounds. On one end of the grounds, he built a dormitory, classroom, library, and office for NEATS. In the middle, he placed a kitchen to feed all the students. Near the kitchen, Seed Effect would use a building for their office, and they experimented with both a sewing school and an internet cafe there as well. Water Harvest, now 4Africa, started their work in South Sudan from a corner of these grounds. And a large soccer (football) field took the space between 4Africa's office and our secondary school.

In Part 1, I told you the story of Moses. While Moses is a composite, everything he did has happened. I even took real people and events to create Beatrice, his mother. Below is what inspired the week with Moses:

Beginning in 2007, a young guy, just like Moses, would come to these grounds to attend NEATS and learn how to pastor and plant churches. He would attend the flagship church on the grounds and witness David Kaya and Edward Dima pastor a large, vibrant, biblically healthy church. David and Edward preached giving, and the church gave enough to pay its pastors and send its own missionaries out.

The young man would attend class during the week. In these classes not only would he survey every book of the Bible, but he would also learn theology, preaching, basic ministry, and, of course, missiology. He would be in at least one small discipleship group. In the evenings and weekends, he would go into the surrounding villages to share the gospel, lead discipleship groups, play the Jesus Film, open-air preach, or lead a Sunday service at a church under a tree. He would participate in at least one church plant as a requirement to graduate.

He might lead devotions at the primary or secondary school. He could join the church choir and learn to lead worship. He'd ride on Edward's motorbike, observing how Edward checked on sick or hurting church members at their homes. He'd watch mature pastors conduct weddings and love people through funerals. In these rituals, he'd watch these pastors navigate allegiance to the Bible over traditional beliefs tied to weddings and funerals that often involved spirit and ancestor worship.

He would get to know Seed Effect and 4Africa and have them expose him to financial empowerment, water well drilling, and healthcare, all in his context.

In 2015, women integrated into NEATS, and today we have an entire women's ministry dedicated to training women as well.

From 2006 to 2016, we didn't fully grasp how powerful a church-planter factory we had in Kajo Keji. We were exposing future church planters to tremendous opportunity all while discipling them and having them experience first-class examples set by David Kaya, Edward Dima, and Kenneth Duku. This ten-year run in an almost accidental incubator would produce our strongest leaders. It inspired us to fully embrace the flagship church vision we would launch in 2021.

I Dreamed I Saw Jesus

By 2021, the South Sudan government army had beaten most of the rebels, and the fighting was cooling off. It was safe enough to return. James and Peter, Monychol's disciples, were among the first refugees to enter the camps in Uganda. They were also among the first to leave. They hated the food in Uganda, life in the camps was draining their souls, and James became ill and weak.

James was convinced the wetter, cooler climate in Uganda was slowly killing him. He left the camp and returned to the Upper Nile. Back in a more arid climate, his health returned, and with his medical training, he quickly secured a job in a health clinic. He also immediately started a church in the community. Good thing he did. God was about to use him.

Abida was a Muslim teenager living in a village near James's clinic and church. Here's her story: "One night I had a very vivid dream," she recounted. "I dreamed I saw Jesus. At the beginning of the dream, Jesus gave me water to drink, then he told me, 'I am the Truth.'"

Her dream continued. "I saw Jesus walking through my village, and everyone in this village was following him."

When she woke up, she told her mother all about the dream. Her mother said, "You are being called by God." Her mother remembered a Christian man who worked in the health clinic: James.

They called James to their home, and he explained who Jesus is. Abida believed fully in the Jesus she'd seen in her dream and now learned more about him from James.

She was so transformed she immediately began sharing about Jesus with other youth and children in the community, and she quickly progressed to teaching them regularly while also still learning herself.

God still sends visions and dreams. He was about to send a big one to David Kaya.

YOU'RE NOT GOING TO LIKE THIS

"M IKE, YOU ARE not going to like this."

That's how David started his call to me in the states. We had been through so many ups and downs over the years that my heart didn't race this time. David didn't wait for me to respond. "I have been up all night talking with God. Mike, we have to put up the cross of Christ in Sudan."

In Sudan, 46.7 million people are unreached, meaning the vast majority of that number have not heard the gospel.[14] I was listening. I wanted to do much more in Sudan to reach these unreached peoples.

David pressed on. "The believers need a refuge. When they come to faith in Christ, their families are kicking them out of their homes. Sometimes they want to kill them. They need a place to run and sleep and live. I know we have said we do not build buildings. Empower One

---

14 "Country: Sudan," Joshua Project, https://joshuaproject.net/countries/SU.

does not build churches or buildings, but, Mike, Sudan is different, and we have to do things differently there."

I still just listened. He was right. We had always refused to build churches. If a local church wanted a building, we encouraged them to build it themselves. I felt almost all church construction stories were bad ones on the mission field.

David continued, "They need schools next to these churches. When they discover believers, they remove their children from school. We need to have schools for these children. We need to drill water wells to provide clean water. And they need clinics. When the believers are discovered, the clinics will not serve them. The sick will die without medication. God is telling me we must put up the cross of Christ in Sudan."

I paused. Our team had been praying for five months before this call. We prayed a simple prayer: "God teach us to abide in you." We dumped outside books, strategies, conferences, and other ministry's methods. We just prayed to abide in God's vine. To just be a branch. I felt like God was telling us what to do next. The plan would come through David.

I responded, "Actually, I totally agree with you."

Eight thousand miles away, I felt David's relief and joy through the phone.

Listening to Persecuted Believers

Two years earlier, I sat in a church in the country of Chad with sixteen men, all Sudanese believers. I asked them, "If you're comfortable, would you share about the persecution you've experienced since following Christ?"

Here is a tiny fraction of the stories they told me:

"I was able to send my family to America. My wife has sent the document that will allow me to join her. But leaders in my community intercepted this letter and are keeping it from me. I haven't seen my family in years, and without that document I may never be able to see them."

"I was placed in prison and beaten so badly I have difficulty with headaches when I'm exposed to light." (He wore sunglasses inside.)

"My wife didn't convert. Her family is trying to take her back and keep her away from me." (They have children.)

"My business was boycotted, and I was forced to sell what little remained."

To a man, they said following Christ was worth it and they'd gladly die for Jesus.

And finally, another man said he had a question for me. "Yes, go ahead," I said.

"Why am I only now learning about Jesus? Why has no one told our people about Jesus for all these years? This land [Sudan] was Christian hundreds of years ago. What happened? Why did no one tell us the truth?"

That question haunted me. With this experience and others, I knew David was right. I sensed his idea was from God, and I agreed.

David then used a phrase I'd heard from him years earlier: "I am thinking these need to be flagship churches. They need to take responsibility for their entire state. I am also thinking we need three." And he named three cities we can't disclose publicly.

The seed God had planted through Harold Cathey was about to sprout.

Vision 2032

After the COVID pandemic, South Sudan wasn't exactly stable, but it was stable enough that David had determined it was time to start moving back. He wanted us to get back to starting churches throughout the country.

"I am not leaving anymore," David told me on a phone call. "We will be like Israel. We will *bring* peace to our area. I am not leaving anymore."

We often don't know what we have until we lose it. A cliche, but a cliche because it's true. We hadn't fully realized how special of an environment we had created at Kajo Keji until we were forced to abandon it and spend over seven years in the refugee camps.

As we thought and prayed about the concept of a flagship church, we kept coming back to what we had experienced in Kajo Keji. We had formed, shaped, and incubated many of our best leaders in that environment. What if we replicated it? This had been David's dream since 2002, but he'd kept it quiet because he felt he lacked support and the resources to attempt it.

On another call, David and I talked about his dream. "Mike, I am thinking we need to put up five more flagship churches in South Sudan in our key areas. We will put up the three in Sudan, and we will put up five in South Sudan in places where we have strong leaders."

I agreed, and our American board of directors backed the plan as well.

"We cannot let this work die after we are gone." Despite David being in his early fifties when he said this, he often spoke as if he was nearing his life's end. He's not, by the way. He's healthy and both his parents are still alive. But after he turned fifty, he began to speak like he was eighty. "We have to have very strong churches that can hold the work together and continue planting more churches and reaching unreached people after we are gone."

David came to America that October to both thank existing partners and to help us raise funds for the ministry. This was our annual pattern. While riding through the back roads of North Carolina in a rented Honda Accord, we polished the plan.

"How much do you think we'll need for these eight flagship churches?" I asked David from the passenger seat.

David sat quietly for a moment in the back seat, then he said, "I think $80,000. I think we can build each church for $80,000."

"Okay, so we need $660,000." I said, "And we still need over $400,000 to finish the year in the black just to run the ministry. What a great opportunity for God. We'll see what happens." I felt confident the project was from God, but I was nervous to make the budget. Sometimes faith is just doing things even, or especially, when you're scared.

Sixty-four days later, God gave us all the funding. We had never raised that much money that quickly. Now it really felt like this project was from God.

In early 2022, we began buying plots of land for the flagship churches, broke ground, and started construction on the two churches in Sudan and one in Nimule, South Sudan. David wanted to start two in Sudan to honor our desire to create these refuges. He chose Nimule in South Sudan for the third site because of its proximity to Uganda. It sits directly on the border. This would enable us to bring materials in from Uganda fairly easily, and we felt we could learn our lessons in the least expensive way possible. We were off and running.

In May, the American side of the team gathered in Dallas for a planning meeting. We went through an exercise where we listed things we'd love to see God do through us in the next ten years. We based this exercise on the idea that we generally overestimate what we can accomplish in one year, and greatly underestimate what we can accomplish in ten years.

David Taylor, who had transitioned from a missions pastor and joined our team about a year earlier, commanded the whiteboard. I only listened to the team. I kept my thumb off the scale. David Taylor solicited the team's ideas and created this bulleted list:

- Mike and Kaya ready to hand off
- [Redacted] becomes Sudan HQ and sends missionaries

- Village sustains ministry: 2,500 villagers [We call our monthly givers "The Village."]
- Every position has a successor, disciple
- Every remaining UPG [unreached people group] in Sudan is touched by Empower One
- Church planting by tree, house, flagship
- Gospel presentations
- 10 NEATS campuses
- People sent to near culture [Near culture means you empower believers from a tribe or group near one that is unreached to go and engage that unreached tribe. The nearness of culture and language is more effective than bringing in an outsider.]
- 10 US legacy churches [These are American churches that would be significant partners to a corresponding African flagship church.]
- 10 healthy, profitable primary schools
- Partner org for schools and water
- African-led US conference
- Mike writes a book

When we felt we'd come to the end of the exercise, David Taylor said, "Mike, I think you should take these, pray over them, and see if you can create a new vision statement from what we've given you today."

What emerged was Vision 2032.

I felt the focus for our next ten years should be ensuring dignity.

Our nonnegotiables remained: bring the gospel to as many unreached people as possible before Jesus comes back, and start new, healthy churches. We further cemented these with a refreshed mission statement from this same meeting.

Vision 2032 would provide our African teammates with the infrastructure to pursue the unreached and start churches entirely with their own, local resources. The final frontier in missions was financial self-sustainability.

Dignity.

I took the bullet points, wrote a vision statement, and sent it to David Kaya. We had to be in total agreement. As evidence of God putting David and me together (and the power of the Holy Spirit), I can't think of a significant issue we've disagreed on in almost twenty years together. And no one would describe either of us as pushovers. In fact, we've both had our share of accusations of the opposite.

David messaged me back that he totally agreed with Vision 2032 and that this is exactly what God wanted us to do next.

Here's what we agreed to, and the American board ratified:

By 2032

We will have fifteen flagship churches that will be church multiplication centers. They will be in South Sudan, Sudan, and DR Congo. Each of these centers will have a mother church with about five hundred members. These members will pay the pastoral staff and send out their own missionaries. Each church will be self-sustained by the local congregation.

By 2032, each flagship church will have planted at least fifty churches in each one's respective geographic area, resulting in seven hundred and fifty total new churches.

Each flagship church will have an accompanying primary school, serving kids from grades one to eight.

Each flagship church will have a NEATS Church-planting Bible School Extension Center training thirty church planters each year in Bible, doctrine, theology, and practical ministry, including evangelism, disciple making, and planting churches.

Each flagship church will have a clean water kiosk.

Each flagship church will have a clinic/pharmacy serving the local community.

Each flagship church will have a radio station providing gospel content, worship music, and discipleship lessons to its surrounding area.

As of this writing, Sudan has 131 unreached people groups, including nine unengaged people groups. We want to be part of a network that touches each of these people groups, and we are praying and hoping Sudan's Christian population will greatly increase from its current 4.99% as of this writing.

Agents of Dignity

Essentially, I want to replicate what we experienced in Kajo Keji. But instead of eight churches, we plan to build and launch fifteen flagship church multiplication centers. We also want to keep the three locations in Sudan and put one in the capital of all ten states in South Sudan, plus Kajo Keji. And, because the DR Congo team is so strong, we want to place a fifteenth in the northeast region of DR Congo.

We see this as an opportunity to be agents of dignity for our friends. No more dependence, no more worrying about "the golden rule" (he who has the gold, rules). Our new vision is for this church network in East Africa to stand on its own.

Here's how we plan to do it. And, yes, we're basing this off a use-case of one. This is what pioneering ministries do. Plus, God is a rewarder of faith (see Heb. 11:6).

The size of the flagship church is intentional. If the pastors of these flagship churches can grow those churches to about five hundred members, and faithfully preach giving, not only can that church support its pastors, but it can also send its own missionaries out.

Prior to the war, our schools were profitable. We intend to network these fifteen schools together into one school system, pool the profits, and use those to partially fund the ministry.

We've also funded the capital and start-up expenses for two pharmacies that never needed additional funds. We expect the fifteen for the flagships to help provide income as well.

I'm writing this two and half years into this vision. In Nimule, we already have the flagship church and school built, and we put up a large water tank as well. Church leaders there began selling water as a revenue stream as well (no pun intended). But don't worry, they make sure to give clean water to the very poor, widows, and orphans for free.

With God's help, by encouraging some of the poorest people on earth to give and by pooling their resources, this network of churches should no longer need support from the Western Church. The $660,000 original project became a $15 million ten-year vision. And with inflation, it may pass that number. But God is generous and good.

As of this writing, we have local leaders already working in thirteen of the fifteen locations. We've purchased plots of land in eight locations. We've completed, or nearly completed, six flagship churches. We have four water systems running, one high school, and one radio station up and going.

In April 2023, Sudan erupted into a civil war, pausing our construction on the first two flagship churches. They've not been harmed. We have a handshake agreement with a sister ministry that if the churches in Sudan are destroyed because of persecution, they'll rebuild them for us. South Sudan is one of the most corrupt, unstable countries on Earth. I know it seems crazy to do this. Some might wonder why we even try. But you can either look at the situation as hopeless and not make a difference at all, or, you can walk by faith, throw your starfish, and maybe one of those kids at that school in Nimule becomes president one day and changes the course of the country.

God Is Fun

One last God story about these flagship churches.

We wanted to build one in Malakal, South Sudan— the home of John, James, and Peter from earlier chapters. We tried to buy a building there unsuccessfully. It's extraordinarily difficult to find (or create) building materials. For example, there's no sand. We started talking about putting all the pieces of the church on a barge in the capital city, Juba, and shipping it up the Nile River. We were stumped.

Then David Kaya walked into a construction company's office in Juba. The owner is a believer. After hearing David's desire to build in Malakal, the owner said, "I put a large amount of building materials in a compound in Malakal in 2009. We were contracted to build a bank that year in the city. The project owner had a lot of problems. Those materials have been sitting there since that time."

God put bricks, steel, sand, and loads of other things in Malakal in 2009 just for us to use in 2024.

Isn't God fun?

Take the Leap

It's time to close this story. I'm writing in a coffee shop in Dallas today. It's called Well Grounded, and they employ women who have been incarcerated to help them transition back to society. It's not about the coffee. It's about dignity. The dignity of a good job where people treat you with respect, you work as a team, and Christ's love and mercy is felt in a practical way.

We all want dignity. It feels good. Not a proud good or a look-at-me good. It's deeper. It comes from a place deep inside us. In our soul. We are image bearers of God. Dignity is one of the places we feel "eternity in our hearts" (Eccl. 3:11). It gives us ballast, makes our feet firm, straightens our spines, and lifts our chins. I am created in God's image. I delight in him and he in me. Our small band of spiritual-limp-walkers at Empower One are hoping God keeps using us to ensure dignity in one of the toughest corners of the world.

Right now in the corner of this coffee shop sits an older man with curly gray hair that flows past his ears. I see him there several days a week playing his acoustic guitar and harmonica, taking requests. At the moment, he's playing and singing "Dust in the Wind" by the band Kansas.

The perfect coda for this story.

"Come now, you who say, 'Today or tomorrow we will go to such and such a city, and spend a year there and engage in business and make a profit.' Yet you do not know what your life will be like tomorrow. You are *just* a vapor that appears for a little while and then vanishes away. Instead, *you ought* to say, "If the Lord wills, we will live and also do this or that."'" (James 4:13–15).

Vapor, fog, mist, dust. Dust in the wind.

I didn't set out to work in South Sudan and Sudan. I didn't know what church planting was, and I never dreamed of starting a seminary and working with churches and people all over America. I don't think I knew where Sudan was on a map. I was a Dockers-wearing drone whose soul was dying and enmeshed in all sorts of sinful messes. I couldn't have imagined that David Kaya's daughter would name her baby after my daughter, Alexa. That my kids would have a second family, a second life, in a place like South Sudan. That I'd baptize people in the same Nile River where Moses dipped his staff.

Embrace being vapor. Let go of this world and her shiny idols. Embrace "If the Lord wills, we'll do this or that." Let God blow you in, around, and through his kingdom. Take your warts, your bomb-outs, your screwups, your weaknesses, and your fears to him. Let him cover you, clean you, and use you more than you could ever imagine.

Take the leap. Ensure dignity. God is fun.

AFTERWORD

Moses

Moses, whom you met in Part 1, is a composite character along with his immediate family. Everyone else in the story is a real person. While Moses and family are composites, everything they did someone has actually done, although perhaps not in one week. And I based who Moses and his mother are on real people I've met and worked with and who live in South Sudan.

Empower One Today

As of this writing, Empower One has started six of the fifteen flagship churches, with four of them complete. We have one high school up and running, four clean water kiosks distributing water near the flagships, and one radio station almost launched. Vision 2032 is on its way.

Aerial view of the first flagship church in Nimule, South Sudan.
The buildings to its right are a high school, or secondary school.

The team is healthy. We're peaceful: everyone helps one another and is for one another. It's a sweet season. Famed management consultant Peter Drucker allegedly is the source for the quote, "Culture eats strategy for breakfast." This has moved from just a quote I had heard to something I now feel in my soul. Further, I now would add that people *are* your culture. As the leader of the American side of Empower One, my creating and then vigilantly guarding and fighting for our culture is, perhaps, my most important job. I'm happy to say, I love our culture today.

I was afraid the flagship churches might provoke jealousy and strife in Africa. The opposite has occurred. It's unified the entire ministry, and instead we're cheering one another on, rejoicing when good things happen to and through our teammates.

If you want to jump in with us or learn more, head over to empower-one.org and get in touch. We'd love to talk.

To My Fellow Nonprofit Executive Directors

A lament and encouragement to my fellow executive directors and parachurch leaders out there: I see you.

You signed up because you love the programs and field ministry and the heart of the work. You're now a fundraiser. You're not alone in the fundraising grind. God bless you for dying to what you want to do for the betterment of your organization. You're doing great work. Yet you continually must *convince* folks you're doing great work. It's exhausting. God sees and knows.

I know you want that board member to advocate more. You know you need to deal with that one employee, but if he or she leaves, you'll have even less help! It's a nonprofit, but you have to run it in the black. Few people understand that. You can't distribute the net revenue, and you're not building anything that you can sell one day. You probably don't have benefits, or they're terrible. Retirement? Are you kidding me? You recruit talent that requires them to raise their own salary or take deep pay cuts. Holding volunteers accountable feels impossible.

God sees and knows.

I see you.

ACKNOWLEDGMENTS

GOD, AS IN the one who includes Jesus and the Holy Spirit: Apart from you, I can do nothing. I don't want to, either. You are actually even *more* than who you say you are. You're always good, often fun, and always faithful. I hope I've represented you well. Life with you has been far richer than I could have ever imagined. I can't wait to see what you have for me next.

Ali: You're the love of my life. We've weathered storms, but you're the only one I'd want to weather them with. And the irony is, as long as we're okay, I don't worry about any outside storms. If I didn't have you, none of this would have happened. Thanks for always saying yes.

David Kaya: I could write an entire book about what you mean to me and how you've impacted my life. Empower One *is* you. I'm glad God partnered us together. It's been a miracle from day one. I hope we're neighbors in heaven.

Alexa, Weston, and Erin Kaya: Thanks for tolerating a dad who left for weeks at a time, multiple times per year. You three were my primary reason for writing this book. I love you guys.

Nathan Sheets: You found David, you helped us start, you taught me how to "do" so much of this, and you've never wavered in your support and friendship. Your fingerprints are all over Empower One.

Matt Jones, Kelly Pearson, and Tammy Lewis: Thanks for not quitting in 2020. I'll always owe you a debt of gratitude for walking through that dark season with me. You've made quite the kingdom impact.

Blake Atwood, my editor and coach: I sat in front of you with twenty-five thousand words and no idea what to do. You completely transformed and reshaped my original idea into something far better than I could have imagined. I could not have done this without you.

Traci Matt, my other editor (I needed two!): Thanks for the encouragement, and for shaping, reshaping, and caring enough to point out several places I might have turned a shade of red had it hit print. And for the nudge for the title.

Trey Hill and Jordan Snowzell: I used several of your photos. Thanks for coming over and using your gifts to bless our ministry.

Scott Crossman: In a literal hallway conversation, you suggested I take my emails and write them as a book. It's stuck with me all these years, and it motivated me. I finally did it.

Timm Sasser: You keep teaching me grace.

Steve G.: It ended poorly, but you were often the invisible hand behind the scenes, and you took the leap with me and helped create Empower One. You deserve recognition.

Blacklist guys: Thanks for the safe outlet every year. I love my brothers. You're each a gift to me . . . except one of you. You know who you are.[15] TBLR.

Empower One's board of directors: Thank you for the unwavering support you've provided me. Your encouragement, oversight, and wise counsel have made this possible.

Churches, partners, donors, friends: I can't list each of you. Actually, I could—I have the records—but it'd be weird. I try to tell you often, but I'm incredibly grateful for you. God has used you more than you can imagine. One day, in glory, he'll show you, and it will blow your minds. Thank you for so many years of encouragement and support.

---

15 Don't worry, dear reader. It's an inside joke. I actually love him.

ABOUT THE AUTHOR

MIKE CONGROVE IS the executive director and cofounder of Empower One, a ministry planting churches across South Sudan, Sudan, Democratic Republic of Congo, northern Uganda, and Chad since 2006. Previously serving as Africa Continent Director at e3 Partners, Mike escaped nine years of corporate drudgery with his soul—and sense of humor—intact. He lives in Texas with his wife Ali and their three children.

You can learn more about Empower One and reach Mike at Empower One's website: empower-one.org.